Je

M000189036

~won,
Israel
and
the Nations

Compiled by

Ruth Ward Heflin

All Scripture quotations are from the Authorized King James
Version of the Bible.

McDougal Publishing is a ministry of The McDougal Foundation, Inc., a Maryland nonprofit corporation dedicated to
spreading the Gospel of the Lord Jesus Christ to as many people
as possible in the shortest time possible.

PUBLISHED BY:

McDOUGAL PUBLISHING
P.O. BOX 3595
HAGERSTOWN, MD 21742-3595
www.mcdougal.org

ISBN 1-884369-65-0

Printed in the United States of America
For Worldwide Distribution

Hardback edition: 1994
Softback edition: 1999

Other books by Ruth Ward Heflin:

Glory
Revival Glory
River Glory

Jerusalem, Zion, Israel and the Nations would not have been possible without the many hours of selfless help by my friend, who also happens to be my publisher, Rev. Harold McDougal.

Ruth Ward Heflin

Contents

God is returning the focus once again to Jerusalem. The place of beginnings is also the place of endings. And God's endings are always glorious.

This overview is by no means definitive but an unfolding of scriptures coming into prominence in these days. As Moses saw the Promised Land from Nebo, one sees the world from Jerusalem.

Ruth Heflin
Jerusalem, Israel

Ezekiel 16:3-14:

Thus saith the Lord God unto JERUSALEM; Thy birth and thy nativity is of the land of Canaan; thy father was an Amorite, and thy mother an Hittite.

And as for thy nativity, in the day thou wast born thy navel was not cut, neither wast thou washed in water to supple thee; thou wast not salted at all, nor swaddled at all.

None eye pitied thee, to do any of these unto thee, to have compassion upon thee; but thou wast cast out in the open field, to the lothing of thy person, in the day that thou wast born.

And when I passed by thee, and saw thee polluted in thine own blood, I said unto thee when thou wast in thy blood, Live; yea, I said unto thee when thou wast in thy blood, Live.

I have caused thee to multiply as the bud of the field, and thou hast increased and waxen great, and thou art come to excellent ornaments: thy breasts are fashioned, and thine hair is grown, whereas thou wast naked and bare.

Now when I passed by thee, and looked upon thee, behold, thy time was the time of love; and I spread my skirt over thee, and covered thy nakedness: yea, I sware unto thee, and entered into a covenant with thee, saith the Lord God, and thou becamest mine.

Then washed I thee with water; yea, I throughly washed away thy blood from thee, and I anointed thee with oil.

I clothed thee also with broidered work, and shod thee with badgers' skin, and I girded thee about with fine linen, and I covered thee with silk.

I decked thee also with ornaments, and I put bracelets upon thy hands, and a chain on thy neck.

And I put a jewel on thy forehead, and earrings in thine ears, and a beautiful crown upon thine head.

Thus wast thou decked with gold and silver; and thy raiment was of fine linen, and silk, and broidered work; thou didst eat fine flour, and honey, and oil: and thou wast exceeding beautiful, and thou didst prosper into a kingdom.

And thy renown went forth among the heathen [THE NATIONS] for thy beauty: for it was perfect through my comeliness, which I had put upon thee, saith the Lord God.

Jerusalem

Psalms 122:1-9:

I Was glad when they said unto me, Let us go into the house of the Lord.

Our feet shall stand within thy gates, O JERUSALEM.

JERUSALEM is builded as a city that is compact together:

Whither the tribes go up, the tribes of the Lord, unto the testimony of Israel, to give thanks unto the name of the Lord.

For there are set thrones of judgment, the thrones of the house of David.

Pray for the peace of JERUSALEM: they shall prosper that love thee.

Peace be within thy walls, and prosperity within thy palaces.

For my brethren and companions' sakes, I will now say, Peace be within thee.

Because of the house of the Lord our God I will seek thy good.

JERUSALEM: Her Names — Past, Present and Future

Aholibah

Ezekiel 23:4:

And the names of them were Aholah the elder, and **Aholibah** her sister: and they were mine, and they bare sons and daughters. Thus were their names; Samaria is Aholah, and JERUSALEM **Aholibah.**

Ariel

Isaiah 29:1:

Ariel, the city where David dwelt!

Isaiah 29:7:

And the multitude of all the nations that fight against **Ariel**, even all that fight against her and her munition, and that distress her, shall be as a dream of a night vision.

The City of David

2 Samuel 6:10:

So David would not remove the ark of the Lord unto him into **the city of David**: but David carried it aside into the house of Obededom the Gittite.

1 Kings 2:10:

So David slept with his fathers, and was buried in **the city of David.**

1 Kings 11:27:

And this was the cause that he lifted up his hand against the king: Solomon built Millo, and repaired the breaches of **the city of David** his father.

1 Chronicles 13:13:

So David brought not the ark home to himself to **the city of David,** but carried it aside into the house of Obededom the Gittite.

2 Chronicles 8:11:

And Solomon brought up the daughter of Pharaoh out of **the city of David** unto the house that he had built for her:

The City of God

Psalms 46:4:

There is a river, the streams whereof shall make glad **the city of God,** the holy place of the tabernacles of the most High.

Psalms 87:3:

Glorious things are spoken of thee, O **city of God**. Selah.

The City of Judah

2 Chronicles 25:28:

And they brought him upon horses, and buried him with his fathers in **the city of Judah.**

The City of Joy

Jeremiah 49:25:

How is the city of praise not left, **the city of my joy!**

The City of Peace

Hebrews 7:2:

To whom also Abraham gave a tenth part of all; first being by interpretation King of righteousness, and after that also King of **Salem**, which is, King of peace;

The City of Praise

Jeremiah 49:25:

How is **the city of praise** not left, the city of my joy!

The City of Righteousness

Isaiah 1:26:

And I will restore thy judges as at the first, and thy counsellors as at the beginning: afterward thou shalt be called, **The city of righteousness,** the faithful city.

The City of Solemnities

Isaiah 33:20:

Look upon Zion, **the city of our solemnities:** thine eyes shall see JERUSALEM a quiet habitation, a tabernacle that shall not be taken down; not one of the stakes thereof shall ever be removed, neither shall any of the cords thereof be broken.

The City of the Great King

Psalms 48:2:

Beautiful for situation, the joy of the whole earth, is mount Zion, on the sides of the north, **the city of the great King.**

Matthew 5:35:

Nor by the earth; for it is his footstool: neither by JERU-SALEM; for it is **the city of the great King.**

The City of the Lord

Isaiah 60:14:

The sons also of them that afflicted thee shall come bending unto thee; and all they that despised thee shall bow themselves down at the soles of thy feet; and they shall call thee; **The city of the Lord,** The Zion of the Holy One of Israel.

A City of Truth

Zechariah 8:3:
Thus saith the Lord; I am returned unto Zion, and will dwell in the midst of JERUSALEM: and JERUSALEM shall be called **a city of truth**; and the mountain of the Lord of hosts the holy mountain.

The Faithful City

Isaiah 1:26:
And I will restore thy judges as at the first, and thy counsellers as at the beginning: afterward thou shalt be called, The city of righteousness, **the faithful city.**

The Gate of My People

Obadiah 1:13:
Thou shouldest not have entered into **the gate of my people** in the day of their calamity;

Micah 1:9:
For her wound is incurable; for it is come unto Judah; he is come unto **the gate of my people,** even to JERUSALEM.

Great Among the Nations

Lamentations 1:1:
How doth the city sit solitary, that was full of people!

how is she become as a widow! she that was **great among the nations**, and princess among the provinces, how is she become tributary!

A Green Olive Tree

Jeremiah 11:16:
The Lord called thy name, **A green olive tree,** fair, and of goodly fruit: with the noise of a great tumult he hath kindled fire upon it, and the branches of it are broken.

Hephzibah

Isaiah 62:4:
Thou shalt no more be termed Forsaken; neither shall thy land any more be termed Desolate: but thou shalt be called **Hephzibah,** and thy land Beulah: for the Lord delighteth in thee, and thy land shall be married.

The Holy City

Nehemiah 11:1:
And the rulers of the people dwelt at JERUSALEM: the rest of the people also cast lots, to bring one of ten to dwell in JERUSALEM **the holy city,** and nine parts to dwell in other cities.

Nehemiah 11:18:
All the Levites in **the holy city** were two hundred fourscore and four.

Isaiah 48:2:

For they call themselves of **the holy city**, and stay themselves upon the God of Israel; the Lord of hosts is his name.

Isaiah 52:1:

Awake, awake; put on thy strength, O Zion; put on thy beautiful garments, O JERUSALEM, **the holy city**: for henceforth there shall no more come into thee the uncircumcised and the unclean.

Matthew 4:5:

Then the devil taketh him up into **the holy city**, and setteth him on a pinnacle of the temple,

Matthew 27:53:

And came out of the graves after his resurrection, and went into **the holy city**, and appeared unto many.

Revelation 11:2:

But the court which is without the temple leave out, and measure it not; for it is given unto the Gentiles: and **the holy city** shall they tread under foot forty and two months.

The Holy Mountain
(My Holy Mountain, The Holy Mountain of God)

Isaiah 11:9:

They shall not hurt nor destroy in all **my holy mountain**: for the earth shall be full of the knowledge of the Lord, as the waters cover the sea.

Isaiah 56:7:

Even them will I bring to **my holy mountain**, and make them joyful in my house of prayer: their burnt offerings and their sacrifices shall be accepted upon mine altar; for mine house shall be called an house of prayer for all people.

Isaiah 57:13:

When thou criest, let thy companies deliver thee; but the wind shall carry them all away; vanity shall take them: but he that putteth his trust in me shall possess the land, and shall inherit **my holy mountain;**

Isaiah 65:25:

The wolf and the lamb shall feed together, and the lion shall eat straw like the bullock: and dust shall be the serpent's meat. They shall not hurt nor destroy in all **my holy mountain**, saith the Lord.

Isaiah 66:20:

And they shall bring all your brethren for an offering unto the Lord out of all nations upon horses, and in chariots, and in litters, and upon mules, and upon swift beasts, to **my holy mountain** JERUSALEM, saith the Lord, as the children of Israel bring an offering in a clean vessel into the house of the Lord.

Ezekiel 20:40:

For in **mine holy mountain**, in the mountain of the height of Israel, saith the Lord God, there shall all the house of Israel, all of them in the land, serve me: there will I accept them, and there will I require your offerings, and the firstfruits of your oblations, with all your holy things.

Daniel 9:16:

O Lord, according to all thy righteousness, I beseech thee, let thine anger and thy fury be turned away from thy city JERUSALEM, **thy holy mountain**: because for our sins, and for the iniquities of our fathers, JERUSALEM and thy people are become a reproach to all that are about us.

Daniel 9:20:

And whiles I was speaking, and praying, and confessing my sin and the sin of my people Israel, and presenting my supplication before the Lord my God for **the holy mountain of my God;**

Joel 2:1:

Blow ye the trumpet in Zion, and sound an alarm in **my holy mountain**: let all the inhabitants of the land tremble: for the day of the Lord cometh, for it is nigh at hand;

Joel 3:17:

So shall ye know that I am the Lord your God dwelling in Zion, **my holy mountain**: then shall JERUSALEM be holy, and there shall no strangers pass through her any more.

Zephaniah 3:11:

In that day shalt thou not be ashamed ... for then I will

take away out of the midst of thee them that rejoice in thy pride, and thou shalt no more be haughty because of **my holy mountain.**

Zechariah 8:3:

Thus saith the Lord; I am returned unto Zion, and will dwell in the midst of JERUSALEM: and JERUSALEM shall be called a city of truth; and the mountain of the Lord of hosts **the holy mountain.**

Holy Temple

Psalms 5:7:

But as for me, I will come into thy house in the multitude of thy mercy: and in thy fear will I worship toward **thy holy temple.**

Psalms 65:4:

Blessed is the man whom thou choosest, and causest to approach unto thee, that he may dwell in thy courts: we shall be satisfied with the goodness of thy house, even of **thy holy temple.**

Psalms 79:1:

O God, the heathen are come into thine inheritance; **thy holy temple** have they defiled; they have laid JERUSALEM on heaps.

Psalms 138:2:

I will worship toward **thy holy temple**, and praise thy

name for thy lovingkindness and for thy truth: for thou hast magnified thy word above all thy name.

Jonah 2:4:

Then I said, I am cast out of thy sight; yet I will look again toward **thy holy temple.**

Jonah 2:7:

When my soul fainted within me I remembered the Lord: and my prayer came in unto thee, into **thine holy temple.**

Micah 1:2:

Hear, all ye people; hearken, O earth, and all that therein is: and let the Lord God be witness against you, the Lord from **his holy temple.**

Habakkuk 2:20:

But the Lord is in **his holy temple**: let all the earth keep silence before him.

Jebus/Jebusi

Joshua 18:28:

And Zelah, Eleph, and **Jebusi**, which is JERUSALEM, Gibeath, and Kirjath; fourteen cities with their villages. This is the inheritance of the children of Benjamin according to their families.

Judges 19:10-11:

But the man would not tarry that night, but he rose up

safely: and this is his name whereby he shall be called, **THE LORD OUR RIGHTEOUSNESS.**

Jeremiah 33:16:
In those days shall Judah be saved, and JERUSALEM shall dwell safely: and this is the name wherewith she shall be called, **The Lord our righteousness.**

The Mountain of the Lord of Hosts

Zechariah 8:3:
Thus saith the Lord; I am returned unto Zion, and will dwell in the midst of JERUSALEM: and JERUSALEM shall be called a city of truth; and **the mountain of the Lord of hosts** the holy mountain.

The Perfection of Beauty

Lamentations 2:15:
All that pass by clap their hands at thee; they hiss and wag their head at the daughter of JERUSALEM, saying, Is this the city that men call **The perfection of beauty**, The joy of the whole earth?

Princess Among the Provinces

Lamentations 1:1:
How doth the city sit solitary, that was full of people! how is she become as a widow! she that was great among the nations, and **princess among the provinces**, how is she become tributary!

Salem

Genesis 14:18:

And Melchizedek king of **Salem** brought forth bread and wine: and he was the priest of the most high God.

Psalms 76:2:

In **Salem** also is his tabernacle, and his dwelling place in Zion.

Hebrews 7:1-2:

For this Melchisedec, king of **Salem**, priest of the most high God, who met Abraham returning from the slaughter of the kings, and blessed him;

To whom also Abraham gave a tenth part of all; first being by interpretation King of righteousness, and after that also King of **Salem**, which is, King of peace;

The Throne of the Lord

Jeremiah 3:17:

At that time they shall call JERUSALEM **the throne of the Lord**; and all the nations shall be gathered unto it, to the name of the Lord, to JERUSALEM:

The Valley of Vision

Isaiah 22:1:

The burden of **the valley of vision**. What aileth thee now, that thou art wholly gone up to the housetops?

Isaiah 22:5:
    For it is a day of trouble, and of treading down, and of perplexity by the Lord God of hosts in **the valley of vision.**

Zion

1 Kings 8:1:
    Then Solomon assembled the elders of Israel, and all the heads of the tribes, the chief of the fathers of the children of Israel, unto king Solomon in JERUSALEM, that they might bring up the ark of the covenant of the Lord out of the city of David, which is **Zion.**

Zechariah 9:13:
    When I have bent Judah for me, filled the bow with Ephraim, and raised up thy sons, O **Zion**, against thy sons, O Greece, and made thee as the sword of a mighty man.

The Zion of the Holy One of Israel

Isaiah 60:14:
    The sons also of them that afflicted thee shall come bending unto thee; and all they that despised thee shall bow themselves down at the soles of thy feet; and they shall call thee; The city of the Lord, **The Zion of the Holy One of Israel.**

JERUSALEM: Her Past

JERUSALEM: A Description of the City

Psalms 48:2:

Beautiful for situation, the joy of the whole earth, is mount Zion, on the sides of the north, the city of the great King.

Psalms 48:12-13:

Walk about Zion, and go round about her: tell the towers thereof.

Mark ye well her bulwarks, consider her palaces; that ye may tell it to the generation following.

Psalms 102:14:

For thy servants take pleasure in her stones, and favour the dust thereof.

Psalms 122:3:

JERUSALEM is builded as a city that is compact together:

Psalms 125:2:

As the mountains are round about JERUSALEM, so the Lord is round about his people from henceforth even for ever.

Song of Songs 6:4:

Thou art beautiful, O my love, as Tirzah, comely as JERUSALEM, terrible as an army with banners.

Isaiah 33:20-21:

Look upon Zion, the city of our solemnities: thine eyes shall see JERUSALEM a quiet habitation, a tabernacle that shall not be taken down; not one of the stakes thereof shall ever be removed, neither shall any of the cords thereof be broken.

But there the glorious Lord will be unto us a place of broad rivers and streams; wherein shall go no galley with oars, neither shall gallant ship pass thereby.

Isaiah 60:18:

Violence shall no more be heard in thy land, wasting nor destruction within thy borders; but thou shalt call thy walls Salvation, and thy gates Praise.

Ezekiel 5:5:

Thus saith the Lord God; This is JERUSALEM: I have set it in the midst of the nations and countries that are round about her.

Micah 4:8:

And thou, O tower of the flock, the strong hold of the daughter of Zion, unto thee shall it come, even the first do-

minion; the kingdom shall come to the daughter of JERUSA-
LEM.

Zecheriah 2:4:

And said unto him, Run, speak to this young man, saying,
JERUSALEM shall be inhabited as towns without walls for
the multitude of men and cattle therein:

JERUSALEM: The Place of David's Capital By Divine Appointment

1 Kings 15:4:

Nevertheless for David's sake did the Lord his God give
him a lamp in JERUSALEM, to set up his son after him, and
to establish JERUSALEM:

2 Kings 19:34:

For I will defend this city, to save it, for mine own sake,
and for my servant David's sake.

2 Chronicles 6:6:

But I have chosen JERUSALEM, that my name might be
there; and have chosen David to be over my people Israel.

2 Chronicles 12:13:

So king Rehoboam strengthened himself in JERUSALEM,
and reigned: for Rehoboam was one and forty years old when
he began to reign, and he reigned seventeen years in JERU-
SALEM, the city which the Lord had chosen out of all the
tribes of Israel, to put his name there. And his mother's name
was Naamah an Ammonitess.

JERUSALEM: The Place That Became the Home of the Levites

1 Chronicles 9:34:
These chief fathers of **the Levites** were chief throughout their generations; these dwelt at JERUSALEM.

JERUSALEM: The Place That Became the Home of the High Priests

John 18:15:
And Simon Peter followed Jesus, and so did another disciple: that disciple was known unto the high priest, and went in with Jesus into the palace of **the high priest.**

JERUSALEM: The Place Where the Feasts Were Observed

Ezekiel 36:38:
As the holy flock, as the flock of JERUSALEM in **her solemn feasts**; so shall the waste cities be filled with flocks of men: and they shall know that I am the Lord.

Deuteronomy 16:16:
Three times in a year shall all thy males appear before the Lord thy God in the place which he shall choose; in the **feast** of unleavened bread, and in the **feast** of weeks, and in the **feast** of tabernacles: and they shall not appear before the Lord empty:

Psalms 122:3-5:

JERUSALEM is builded as a city that is compact together:

Whither the tribes go up, the tribes of the Lord, unto the testimony of Israel, to give thanks unto the name of the Lord.

Luke 2:41:

Now his parents went to JERUSALEM every year at the **feast** of the passover.

John 4:20:

Our fathers worshipped in this mountain; and ye say, that in JERUSALEM is the place where men ought to worship.

John 5:1:

After this there was a feast of the Jews; and Jesus went up to JERUSALEM.

John 7:2, 10-11 & 14:

Now the Jews' **feast** of tabernacles was at hand.

But when his brethren were gone up, then went he also up unto the **feast**, not openly, but as it were in secret.

Then the Jews sought him at the **feast**, and said, Where is he?

Now about the midst of the **feast** Jesus went up into the temple, and taught.

John 10:22-23:

And it was at JERUSALEM the **feast** of the dedication, and it was winter.

And Jesus walked in the temple in Solomon's porch.

John 12:20:

And there were certain Greeks among them that came up to worship at the **feast:**

Acts 18:21:

But [Paul] bade them farewell, saying, I must by all means keep this **feast** that cometh in JERUSALEM: but I will return again unto you, if God will. And he sailed from Ephesus.

JERUSALEM: The Place Toward Which God's People Prayed

1 Kings 8:38:

What prayer and supplication soever be made by any man, or by all thy people Israel, which shall know every man the plague of his own heart, and spread forth his hands **toward this house:**

Daniel 6:10:

Now when Daniel knew that the writing was signed, he went into his house; and his windows being open in his chamber **toward JERUSALEM,** he kneeled upon his knees three times a day, and prayed, and gave thanks before his God, as he did aforetime.

JERUSALEM: The Place God's People Have Always Loved

Nehemiah 1:2-4:

Hanani, one of my brethren, came, he and certain men of Judah; and I asked them concerning the Jews that had escaped, which were left of the captivity, and concerning JERU-SALEM.

And they said unto me, The remnant that are left of the captivity there in the province are in great affliction and reproach: the wall of JERUSALEM also is broken down, and the gates thereof are burned with fire.

And it came to pass, when I heard these words, that I sat down and wept, and mourned certain days, and fasted, and prayed before the God of heaven,

Nehemiah 2:5-6:

And I said unto the king, If it please the king, and if thy servant have found favour in thy sight, that thou wouldest send me unto Judah, unto the city of my fathers' sepulchres, that I may build it.

So it pleased the king to send me; and I set him a time.

Psalms 122:6:

Pray for the peace of JERUSALEM: they shall prosper that love thee.

Psalms 137:5-6:

If I forget thee, O JERUSALEM, let my right hand forget her cunning.

If I do not remember thee, let my tongue cleave to the roof of my mouth; if I prefer not JERUSALEM above my chief joy.

Isaiah 62:1:

For Zion's sake will I not hold my peace, and for JERU-

SALEM's sake I will not rest, until the righteousness thereof go forth as brightness, and the salvation thereof as a lamp that burneth.

Isaiah 66:10:

Rejoice ye with JERUSALEM, and be glad with her, all ye that love her: rejoice for joy with her, all ye that mourn for her:

Luke 19:41-42 & 45:

And when he was come near, he beheld the city, and wept over it,

Saying, If thou hadst known, even thou, at least in this thy day, the things which belong unto thy peace!

JERUSALEM: The Place Used By Some In Oaths

Matthew 5:34-35:

But I say unto you, Swear not at all; neither by heaven; for it is God's throne: Nor by the earth; for it is his footstool: neither by JERUSALEM; for it is the city of the great King.

JERUSALEM: The Place That Was Home to Melchizedek, the Ancient King and Priest

Genesis 14:18:

And Melchizedek king of SALEM brought forth bread and wine: and he was the priest of the most high God.

JERUSALEM: The Place First Conquered By David and Established By Him As a Citadel

2 Samuel 5:5, 7 & 9:

In Hebron he reigned over Judah seven years and six months: and in JERUSALEM he reigned thirty and three years over all Israel and Judah.

David took the strong hold of Zion: the same is the city of David.

So David dwelt in the fort, and called it the city of David. And David built round about from Millo and inward.

1 Chronicles 11:7:

And David dwelt in the castle; therefore they called it the city of David.

JERUSALEM: The Place That Became Home to the Ark of the Covenant

2 Samuel 6:12:

And it was told king David, saying, The Lord hath blessed the house of Obededom, and all that pertaineth unto him, because of the ark of God. So David went and brought up the ark of God from the house of Obededom into the city of David with gladness.

JERUSALEM: The Place That David Purchased and Built An Altar to God

2 Samuel 24:19-21:

And Gad came that day to David, and said unto him, Go

up, rear an altar unto the Lord in the threshingfloor of Araunah the Jebusite.

And David, according to the saying of Gad, went up as the Lord commanded.

And Araunah looked, and saw the king and his servants coming on toward him: and Araunah went out, and bowed himself before the king on his face upon the ground.

And Araunah said, Wherefore is my lord the king come to his servant? And David said, To buy the threshingfloor of thee, to build an altar unto the Lord, that the plague may be stayed from the people.

JERUSALEM: The Place Where David Built His Capital Around the Existing Citadel

1 Chronicles 11:8:
And he built the city round about, even from Millo round about: and Joab repaired the rest of the city.

JERUSALEM: The Place Fortified by Solomon

1 Kings 3:1:
And Solomon made affinity with Pharaoh king of Egypt, and took Pharaoh's daughter, and brought her into the city of David, until he had made an end of building his own house, and the house of the Lord, and the wall of JERUSALEM round about.

JERUSALEM: The Place Where the Temple Was Built

David wanted to build the first Temple.

2 Samuel 7:2-3:

That the king said unto Nathan the prophet, See now, I dwell in an house of cedar, but the ark of God dwelleth within curtains.

And Nathan said to the king, Go, do all that is in thine heart; for the Lord is with thee.

1 Chronicles 22:7:

And David said to Solomon, My son, as for me, it was in my mind to build an house unto the name of the Lord my God:

1 Chronicles 28:2:

Then David the king stood up upon his feet, and said, Hear me, my brethren, and my people: as for me, I had in mine heart to build an house of rest for the ark of the covenant of the Lord, and for the footstool of our God, and had made ready for the building:

Psalms 132:2-5:

How he sware unto the Lord, and vowed unto the mighty God of Jacob;

Surely I will not come into the tabernacle of my house, nor go up into my bed;

I will not give sleep to mine eyes, or slumber to mine eyelids,

Until I find out a place for the Lord, an habitation for the mighty God of Jacob.

Acts 7:46:

Who found favour before God, and desired to find a tabernacle for the God of Jacob.

But David was forbidden by God to build the Temple because he was a man of war.

1 Kings 5:3:

Thou knowest how that David my father could not build an house unto the name of the Lord his God for the wars which were about him on every side, until the Lord put them under the soles of his feet.

1 Chronicles 22:7-8:

And David said to Solomon, My son, as for me, it was in my mind to build an house unto the name of the Lord my God:

But the word of the Lord came to me, saying, Thou hast shed blood abundantly, and hast made great wars: thou shalt not build an house unto my name, because thou hast shed much blood upon the earth in my sight.

The building of the Temple was committed to Solomon, David's son.

2 Samuel 7:12:

And when thy days be fulfilled, and thou shalt sleep with thy fathers, I will set up thy seed after thee, which shall proceed out of thy bowels, and I will establish his kingdom.

He shall build an house for my name, and I will stablish the throne of his kingdom for ever.

David, nevertheless, prepared the building site and many of the materials for construction of the Temple and instructed Solomon in their use.

1 Chronicles 22:5:

And David said, Solomon my son is young and tender, and the house that is to be builded for the Lord must be exceeding magnifical, of fame and of glory throughout all countries: I will therefore now make preparation for it. So David prepared abundantly before his death.

1 Chronicles 28:14:

He gave of gold by weight for things of gold, for all instruments of all manner of service; silver also for all instruments of silver by weight, for all instruments of every kind of service:

1 Chronicles 29:2:

Now I have prepared with all my might for the house of my God the gold for things to be made of gold, and the silver for things of silver, and the brass for things of brass, the iron for things of iron, and wood for things of wood; onyx stones, and stones to be set, glistering stones, and of divers colours, and all manner of precious stones, and marble stones in abundance.

And Solomon built the great Temple.

2 Chronicles 3:1:

Then Solomon began to build the house of the Lord at

JERUSALEM in mount Moriah, where the Lord appeared unto David his father, in the place that David had prepared in the threshingfloor of Ornan the Jebusite.

2 Chronicles 5:1:

Thus all the work that Solomon made for the house of the Lord was finished: and Solomon brought in all the things that David his father had dedicated; and the silver, and the gold, and all the instruments, put he among the treasures of the house of God.

Acts 7:47:

But Solomon built him an house.

The Greatness of the Temple

2 Chronicles 2:5-6:

And the house which I build is great: for great is our God above all gods.

But who is able to build him an house, seeing the heaven and heaven of heavens cannot contain him? who am I then, that I should build him an house, save only to burn sacrifice before him?

The Beauty of the Temple

Psalms 27:4:

One thing have I desired of the Lord, that will I seek after; that I may dwell in the house of the Lord all the days of my life, to behold the beauty of the Lord, and to inquire in his temple.

Isaiah 64:11:

Our holy and our beautiful house, where our fathers praised thee.

The Holiness of the Temple

1 Kings 8:10:

And it came to pass, when the priests were come out of the holy place, that the cloud filled the house of the Lord,

1 Kings 9:3:

And the Lord said unto him, I have heard thy prayer and thy supplication, that thou hast made before me: I have hallowed this house, which thou hast built, to put my name there for ever; and mine eyes and mine heart shall be there perpetually.

Matthew 23:17:

Whether is greater, the gold, or **the temple** that sanctifieth the gold?

Jesus and the Temple

Luke 2:22-23:

And when the days of her purification according to the law of Moses were accomplished, they brought him to JERUSALEM, to present him to the Lord;

Luke 2:41-43 & 46:

Now his parents went to JERUSALEM every year at the feast of the passover.

And when he was twelve years old, they went up to JE-RUSALEM after the custom of the feast.

And when they had fulfilled the days, as they returned, the child Jesus tarried behind in JERUSALEM; and Joseph and his mother knew not of it.

And it came to pass, that after three days they found him in **the temple**, sitting in the midst of the doctors, both hearing them, and asking them questions.

Matthew 21:14:

And the blind and the lame came to him in **the temple;** and he healed them.

Luke 19:47:

And he taught daily in **the temple.**

The Names of the Temple

<u>The Temple of the Lord</u>

2 Kings 11:10:

And to the captains over hundreds did the priest give king David's spears and shields, that were in **the temple of the Lord.**

<u>Thy Holy Temple</u>

Psalms 79:1:

O God, the heathen are come into thine inheritance; **thy**

holy temple have they defiled; they have laid JERUSALEM on heaps.

The Holy House

1 Chronicles 29:3:
Moreover, because I have set my affection to the house of my God, I have of mine own proper good, of gold and silver, which I have given to the house of my God, over and above all that I have prepared for **the holy house.**

The House of God

1 Chronicles 29:2:
Now I have prepared with all my might for **the house of my God.**

2 Chronicles 23:9:
Moreover Jehoiada the priest delivered to the captains of hundreds spears, and bucklers, and shields, that had been king David's, which were in **the house of God.**

The House of the Lord

2 Chronicles 23:5:
And a third part shall be at the king's house; and a third part at the gate of the foundation: and all the people shall be in the courts of **the house of the Lord.**

Jeremiah 28:5:
Then the prophet Jeremiah said unto the prophet

Hananiah in the presence of the priests, and in the presence of all the people that stood in **the house of the Lord,**

My Father's House

John 2:16:
And said unto them that sold doves, Take these things hence; make not **my Father's house** an house of merchandise.

The House of the God of Jacob

Isaiah 2:3:
And many people shall go and say, Come ye, and let us go up to the mountain of the Lord, to **the house of the God of Jacob**; and he will teach us of his ways, and we will walk in his paths: for out of Zion shall go forth the law, and the word of the Lord from JERUSALEM.

The House of My Glory

Isaiah 60:7:
All the flocks of Kedar shall be gathered together unto thee, the rams of Nebaioth shall minister unto thee: they shall come up with acceptance on mine altar, and I will glorify **the house of my glory.**

House of Prayer

Isaiah 56:7:
Even them will I bring to my holy mountain, and make

them joyful in **my house of prayer**: their burnt offerings and their sacrifices shall be accepted upon mine altar; for mine house shall be called **an house of prayer** for all people.

Matthew 21:13:

And said unto them, It is written, My house shall be called **the house of prayer**; but ye have made it a den of thieves.

House of Sacrifice

2 Chronicles 7:12:

And the Lord appeared to Solomon by night, and said unto him, I have heard thy prayer, and have chosen this place to myself for **an house of sacrifice**.

House of Their Sanctuary

2 Chronicles 36:17:

Therefore he brought upon them the king of the Chaldees, who slew their young men with the sword in **the house of their sanctuary**, and had no compassion upon young man or maiden, old man, or him that stooped for age: he gave them all into his hand.

Our Holy and Beautiful House

Isaiah 64:11:

Our holy and our beautiful house, where our fathers praised thee,

The Holy Mount

Isaiah 27:13:

And it shall come to pass in that day, that the great trumpet shall be blown, and they shall come which were ready to perish in the land of Assyria, and the outcasts in the land of Egypt, and shall worship the Lord in **the holy mount** at JERUSALEM.

The Mountain of the Lord's House

Isaiah 2:2:

And it shall come to pass in the last days, that **the mountain of the Lord's house** shall be established in the top of the mountains, and shall be exalted above the hills; and all nations shall flow unto it.

The Palace

1 Chronicles 29:1:

Furthermore David the king said unto all the congregation, Solomon my son, whom alone God hath chosen, is yet young and tender, and the work is great: for **the palace** is not for man, but for the Lord God.

1 Chronicles 29:19:

And give unto Solomon my son a perfect heart, to keep thy commandments, thy testimonies, and thy statutes, and to do all these things, and to build **the palace**, for the which I have made provision.

Psalms 122:7:

Peace be within thy walls, and prosperity within thy palaces.

A Sanctuary

2 Chronicles 20:8:

And they dwelt therein, and have built thee **a sanctuary** therein for thy name,

The Tabernacle of Witness

2 Chronicles 24:6:

And the king called for Jehoiada the chief, and said unto him, Why hast thou not required of the Levites to bring in out of Judah and out of JERUSALEM the collection, according to the commandment of Moses the servant of the Lord, and of the congregation of Israel, for **the tabernacle of witness?**

Zion

Psalms 20:2:

Send thee help from the sanctuary, and strengthen thee out of **Zion;**

Psalms 48:12:

Walk about **Zion,** and go round about her: tell the towers thereof.

Psalms 74:2:

Remember thy congregation, which thou hast purchased

of old; the rod of thine inheritance, which thou hast redeemed; this mount **Zion**, wherein thou hast dwelt.

Psalms 87:2:

The Lord loveth the gates of **Zion** more than all the dwellings of Jacob.

Isaiah 2:3:

And many people shall go and say, Come ye, and let us go up to the mountain of the Lord, to the house of the God of Jacob; and he will teach us of his ways, and we will walk in his paths: for out of **Zion** shall go forth the law, and the word of the Lord from JERUSALEM.

JERUSALEM: The Place of Ancient Gates

Psalms 9:14:

That I may shew forth all thy praise in **the gates** of the daughter of Zion: I will rejoice in thy salvation.

Psalms 24:7-10:

Lift up your heads, O ye **gates**; and be ye lift up, ye everlasting doors; and the King of glory shall come in.

Who is this King of glory? The Lord strong and mighty, the Lord mighty in battle.

Lift up your heads, O ye **gates**; even lift them up, ye everlasting doors; and the King of glory shall come in.

Who is this King of glory? The Lord of hosts, he is the King of glory. Selah.

Psalms87:2:

The Lord loveth **the gates** of Zion more than all the dwellings of Jacob.

Psalms 100:4:

Enter into **his gates** with thanksgiving, and into his courts with praise: be thankful unto him, and bless his name.

Psalms 118:19:

Open to me the **gates** of righteousness: I will go into them, and I will praise the Lord:

Isaiah 60:18:

Violence shall no more be heard in thy land, wasting nor destruction within thy borders; but thou shalt call thy walls Salvation, and thy **gates** Praise.

The Valley Gate

Nehemiah 2:13:

And I went out by night by **the gate of the valley**, even before the dragon well, and to the dung port, and viewed the walls of JERUSALEM, which were broken down, and the gates thereof were consumed with fire.

Nehemiah 3:13:

The valley gate repaired Hanun, and the inhabitants of Zanoah; they built it, and set up the doors thereof, the locks thereof, and the bars thereof, and a thousand cubits on the wall unto the dung gate.

The Fountain Gate

Nehemiah 2:14:

Then I went on to **the gate of the fountain**, and to the king's pool: but there was no place for the beast that was under me to pass.

Nehemiah 3:15:

But **the gate of the fountain** repaired Shallun the son of Colhozeh, the ruler of part of Mizpah; he built it, and covered it, and set up the doors thereof, the locks thereof, and the bars thereof, and the wall of the pool of Siloah by the king's garden, and unto the stairs that go down from the city of David.

Nehemiah 12:37:

And at **the fountain gate**, which was over against them, they went up by the stairs of the city of David, at the going up of the wall, above the house of David, even unto the water gate eastward.

The Sheep Gate

Nehemiah 3:1:

Then Eliashib the high priest rose up with his brethren the priests, and they builded **the sheep gate**; they sanctified it, and set up the doors of it; even unto the tower of Meah they sanctified it, unto the tower of Hananeel.

Nehemiah 12:39:

And from above the gate of Ephraim, and above the old

gate, and above the fish gate, and the tower of Hananeel, and the tower of Meah, even unto **the sheep gate**: and they stood still in the prison gate.

The Fish Gate

Nehemiah 3:3:
But **the fish gate** did the sons of Hassenaah build, who also laid the beams thereof, and set up the doors thereof, the locks thereof, and the bars thereof.

Nehemiah 12:39:
And from above the gate of Ephraim, and above the old gate, and above **the fish gate**, and the tower of Hananeel, and the tower of Meah, even unto the sheep gate: and they stood still in the prison gate.

The Old Gate

Nehemiah 3:6:
Moreover **the old gate** repaired Jehoiada the son of Paseah, and Meshullam the son of Besodeiah; they laid the beams thereof, and set up the doors thereof.

Nehemiah 12:39:
And from above the gate of Ephraim, and above **the old gate,** and above the fish gate, and the tower of Hananeel, and the tower of Meah, even unto the sheep gate:

The Dung Gate

Nehemiah 2:13:
And I went out by night by the gate of the valley, even before the dragon well, and to **the dung port**, and viewed the walls of JERUSALEM, which were broken down, and the gates thereof were consumed with fire.

Nehemiah 3:14:
But **the dung gate** repaired Malchiah the son of Rechab, the ruler of part of Bethhaccerem; he built it, and set up the doors thereof, the locks thereof, and the bars thereof.

Nehemiah 12:31:
Then I brought up the princes of Judah upon the wall, and appointed two great companies of them that gave thanks, whereof one went on the right hand upon the wall toward **the dung gate:**

The Water Gate

Nehemiah 3:26:
Moreover the Nethinims dwelt in Ophel, unto the place over against **the water gate** toward the east, and the tower that lieth out.

The Horse Gate

Nehemiah 3:28:
From above **the horse gate** repaired the priests, every one over against his house.

The East Gate

Nehemiah 3:29:

After them repaired Zadok the son of Immer over against his house. After him repaired also Shemaiah the son of Shechaniah, the keeper of **the east gate.**

The Miphkad Gate

Nehemiah 3:31:

After him repaired Malchiah the goldsmith's son unto the place of the Nethinims, and of the merchants, over against **the gate Miphkad**, and to the going up of the corner.

The Ephraim Gate

2 Kings 14:13:

And Jehoash king of Israel took Amaziah king of Judah, the son of Jehoash the son of Ahaziah, at Bethshemesh, and came to JERUSALEM, and brake down the wall of JERUSALEM from **the gate of Ephraim** unto the corner gate, four hundred cubits.

Nehemiah 8:16:

So the people went forth, and brought them, and made themselves booths, every one upon the roof of his house, and in their courts, and in the courts of the house of God, and in the street of the water gate, and in the street of **the gate of Ephraim.**

Nehemiah 12:39:

And from above **the gate of Ephraim**, and above the old

gate, and above the fish gate, and the tower of Hananeel, and the tower of Meah, even unto the sheep gate: and they stood still in the prison gate.

The Prison Gate

Nehemiah 12:39:
And from above the gate of Ephraim, and above the old gate, and above the fish gate, and the tower of Hananeel, and the tower of Meah, even unto the sheep gate: and they stood still in **the prison gate.**

The Benjamin Gate

Jeremiah 37:13:
And when he was in **the gate of Benjamin,** a captain of the ward was there, whose name was Irijah, the son of Shelemiah, the son of Hananiah;

Zechariah 14:10:
All the land shall be turned as a plain from Geba to Rimmon south of JERUSALEM: and it shall be lifted up, and inhabited in her place, from **Benjamin's gate** unto the place of the first gate, unto the corner gate, and from the tower of Hananeel unto the king's winepresses.

The King's Gate

1 Chronicles 9:18:
Who hitherto waited in **the king's gate** eastward: they were porters in the companies of the children of Levi.

The Shallecheth Gate

1 Chronicles 26:16:

To Shuppim and Hosah the lot came forth westward, with **the gate Shallecheth,** by the causeway of the going up, ward against ward.

The High Gate

2 Chronicles 23:20:

And he took the captains of hundreds, and the nobles, and the governors of the people, and all the people of the land, and brought down the king from the house of the Lord: and they came through **the high gate** into the king's house, and set the king upon the throne of the kingdom.

The Middle Gate

Jeremiah 39:3:

And all the princes of the king of Babylon came in, and sat in **the middle gate,** even Nergalsharezer, Samgarnebo, Sarsechim, Rabsaris, Nergalsharezer, Rabmag, with all the residue of the princes of the king of Babylon.

The First Gate

Zechariah 14:10:

All the land shall be turned as a plain from Geba to Rimmon south of JERUSALEM: and it shall be lifted up, and inhabited in her place, from Benjamin's gate unto the place of the first gate, unto the corner gate, and from the tower of Hananeel unto the king's winepresses.

The Gates of Ezekiel's Vision

Ezekiel 48:31-34:

And **the gates** of the city shall be after the names of the tribes of Israel: three **gates** northward; one **gate of Reuben,** one **gate of Judah,** one **gate of Levi.**

And at the east side four thousand and five hundred: and three **gates**; and one **gate of Joseph,** one **gate of Benjamin,** one **gate of Dan.**

And at the south side four thousand and five hundred measures: and three **gates**; one **gate of Simeon,** one **gate of Issachar,** one **gate of Zebulun.**

At the west side four thousand and five hundred, with their three **gates**; one **gate of Gad,** one **gate of Asher,** one gate of **Naphtali.**

The Gates of John's Vision

Revelation 21:12-13, 15 21 & 25:

And had a wall great and high, and had twelve **gates,** and at the **gates** twelve angels, and names written thereon, which are the names of the twelve tribes of the children of Israel:

On the east three **gates**; on the north three **gates**; on the south three **gates**; and on the west three **gates.**

And he that talked with me had a golden reed to measure the city, and the **gates** thereof, and the wall thereof.

And the twelve **gates** were twelve pearls: every several **gate** was of one pearl:

And the **gates** of it shall not be shut at all by day: for there shall be no night there.

JERUSALEM: The Place From Which the Word Would Go Forth

Micah 4:2:

And many nations shall come, and say, Come, and let us go up to the mountain of the Lord, and to the house of the God of Jacob; and he will teach us of his ways, and we will walk in his paths: for **the law shall go forth** of Zion, and the word of the Lord from JERUSALEM.

Luke 24:47:

And that repentance and remission of sins should be preached in his name among all nations, beginning at JERU-SALEM.

JERUSALEM: The Place Where the Holy Spirit Was Outpoured

Luke 24:49:

And, behold, I send the promise of my Father upon you: but tarry ye in the city of JERUSALEM, until ye be endued with power from on high.

Acts 1:4:

And, being assembled together with them, commanded

them that they should not depart from JERUSALEM, but wait for the promise of the Father, which, saith he, ye have heard of me.

Acts 2:1-4:

And when the day of Pentecost was fully come, they were all with one accord in one place.

And suddenly there came a sound from heaven as of a rushing mighty wind, and it filled all the house where they were sitting.

And there appeared unto them cloven tongues like as of fire, and it sat upon each of them.

And they were all filled with the Holy Ghost, and began to speak with other tongues, as the Spirit gave them utterance.

JERUSALEM:
Her Present and Her Future

JERUSALEM: Her Rebuilding and Restoration

From Isaiah

Isaiah 1:26:
And I will restore thy judges as at the first, and thy counsellors as at the beginning: afterward thou shalt be called, The city of righteousness, the faithful city.

Isaiah 11:12:
And he shall set up an ensign for the nations, and shall assemble the outcasts of Israel, and gather together the dispersed of Judah from the four corners of the earth.

Isaiah 44:28:
That saith of Cyrus, He is my shepherd, and shall perform all my pleasure: even saying to JERUSALEM, Thou shalt be built; and to the temple, Thy foundation shall be laid.

Isaiah 60:10:

And the sons of strangers shall build up thy walls, and their kings shall minister unto thee: for in my wrath I smote thee, but in my favour have I had mercy on thee.

From Jeremiah

Jeremiah 31:38-40:

Behold, the days come, saith the Lord, that the city shall be built to the Lord from the tower of Hananeel unto the gate of the corner.

And the measuring line shall yet go forth over against it upon the hill Gareb, and shall compass about to Goath.

And the whole valley of the dead bodies, and of the ashes, and all the fields unto the brook of Kidron, unto the corner of the horse gate toward the east, shall be holy unto the Lord; it shall not be plucked up, nor thrown down any more for ever.

Jeremiah 33:10-11:

Thus saith the Lord; Again there shall be heard in this place, which ye say shall be desolate without man and without beast, even in the cities of Judah, and in the streets of JERUSALEM, that are desolate, without man, and without inhabitant, and without beast,

The voice of joy, and the voice of gladness, the voice of the bridegroom, and the voice of the bride, the voice of them that shall say, Praise the Lord of hosts: for the Lord is good; for his mercy endureth for ever: and of them that shall bring the sacrifice of praise into the house of the Lord. For I will cause to return the captivity of the land, as at the first, saith the Lord.

From Ezekiel

Ezekiel 20:40:

For in mine holy mountain, in the mountain of the height of Israel, saith the Lord God, there shall all the house of Israel, all of them in the land, serve me: there will I accept them, and there will I require your offerings, and the firstfruits of your oblations, with all your holy things.

Ezekiel 36:8:

But ye, O mountains of Israel, ye shall shoot forth your branches, and yield your fruit to my people of Israel; for they are at hand to come.

From Daniel

Daniel 9:25:

Know therefore and understand, that from the going forth of the commandment to restore and to build JERUSALEM unto the Messiah the Prince shall be seven weeks, and threescore and two weeks: the street shall be built again, and the wall, even in troublous times.

From Joel

Joel 3:20-21:

But Judah shall dwell for ever, and JERUSALEM from generation to generation.

For I will cleanse their blood that I have not cleansed: for the Lord dwelleth in Zion.

From Zechariah

Zechariah 1:17:

Cry yet, saying, Thus saith the Lord of hosts; My cities through prosperity shall yet be spread abroad; and the Lord shall yet comfort Zion, and shall yet choose JERUSALEM.

Zechariah 2:1-5:

I Lifted up mine eyes again, and looked, and behold a man with a measuring line in his hand.

Then said I, Whither goest thou? And he said unto me, To measure JERUSALEM, to see what is the breadth thereof, and what is the length thereof.

And, behold, the angel that talked with me went forth, and another angel went out to meet him,

And said unto him, Run, speak to this young man, saying, JERUSALEM shall be inhabited as towns without walls for the multitude of men and cattle therein:

For I, saith the Lord, will be unto her a wall of fire round about, and will be the glory in the midst of her.

Zechariah 8:15:

So again have I thought in these days to do well unto JERUSALEM and to the house of Judah: fear ye not.

Zechariah 10:6:

And I will strengthen the house of Judah, and I will save the house of Joseph, and I will bring them again to place them; for I have mercy upon them: and they shall be as though I had not cast them off: for I am the Lord their God, and will hear them.

Zechariah 14:10:

All the land shall be turned as a plain from Geba to Rimmon south of JERUSALEM: and it shall be lifted up, and inhabited in her place, from Benjamin's gate unto the place of the first gate, unto the corner gate, and from the tower of Hananeel unto the king's winepresses.

From Malachi

Malachi 3:4:

Then shall the offering of Judah and JERUSALEM be pleasant unto the Lord, as in the days of old, and as in former years.

From Jesus

Luke 21:24:

And they shall fall by the edge of the sword, and shall be led away captive into all nations: and JERUSALEM shall be trodden down of the Gentiles, until the times of the Gentiles be fulfilled.

JERUSALEM: Future Capital of Messiah's Eternal Kingdom

Isaiah 2:1-5:

The word that Isaiah the son of Amoz saw concerning Judah and JERUSALEM.

And it shall come to pass in the last days, that the mountain of the Lord's house shall be established in the top of the mountains, and shall be exalted above the hills; and all nations shall flow unto it.

And many people shall go and say, Come ye, and let us go up to the mountain of the Lord, to the house of the God of Jacob; and he will teach us of his ways, and we will walk in his paths: for out of Zion shall go forth the law, and the word of the Lord from JERUSALEM.

And he shall judge among the nations, and shall rebuke many people: and they shall beat their swords into plowshares, and their spears into pruninghooks: nation shall not lift up sword against nation, neither shall they learn war any more.

O house of Jacob, come ye, and let us walk in the light of the Lord.

Joel 3:1:

For, behold, in those days, and in that time, when I shall bring again the captivity of Judah and JERUSALEM,

Joel 3:17-18:

So shall ye know that I am the Lord your God dwelling in Zion, my holy mountain: then shall JERUSALEM be holy, and there shall no strangers pass through her any more.

And it shall come to pass in that day, that the mountains shall drop down new wine, and the hills shall flow with milk, and all the rivers of Judah shall flow with waters, and a fountain shall come forth of the house of the Lord, and shall water the valley of Shittim.

Amos 9:9 & 11:

For, lo, I will command, and I will sift the house of Israel among all nations, like as corn is sifted in a sieve, yet shall not the least grain fall upon the earth.

In that day will I raise up the tabernacle of David that is fallen, and close up the breaches thereof; and I will raise up his ruins, and I will build it as in the days of old:

Amos 9:14-15:

And I will bring again the captivity of my people of Israel, and they shall build the waste cities, and inhabit them; and they shall plant vineyards, and drink the wine thereof; they shall also make gardens, and eat the fruit of them.

And I will plant them upon their land, and they shall no more be pulled up out of their land which I have given them, saith the Lord thy God.

Obadiah 1:17:

But upon mount Zion shall be deliverance, and there shall be holiness; and the house of Jacob shall possess their possessions.

Zechariah 14:8:

And it shall be in that day, that living waters shall go out from JERUSALEM; half of them toward the former sea, and half of them toward the hinder sea: in summer and in winter shall it be.

Zechariah 14:10-11:

All the land shall be turned as a plain from Geba to Rimmon south of JERUSALEM: and it shall be lifted up, and inhabited in her place, from Benjamin's gate unto the place of the first gate, unto the corner gate, and from the tower of Hananeel unto the king's winepresses.

And men shall dwell in it, and there shall be no more utter destruction; but JERUSALEM shall be safely inhabited.

JERUSALEM: The Eternal City

Jeremiah 17:25:

Then shall there enter into the gates of this city kings and princes sitting upon the throne of David, riding in chariots and on horses, they, and their princes, the men of Judah, and the inhabitants of JERUSALEM: and this city shall remain for ever.

Ezekiel 37:25:

And they shall dwell in the land that I have given unto Jacob my servant, wherein your fathers have dwelt; and they shall dwell therein, even they, and their children, and their children's children for ever: and my servant David shall be their prince for ever.

Ezekiel 37:28:

And the heathen shall know that I the Lord do sanctify Israel, when my sanctuary shall be in the midst of them for evermore.

JERUSALEM: The Heavenly City

Galatians 4:26:

But JERUSALEM which is above is free, which is the mother of us all.

Hebrews 11:10 & 16:

For he looked for a city which hath foundations, whose builder and maker is God.

But now they desire a better country, that is, an heavenly: wherefore God is not ashamed to be called their God: for he hath prepared for them a city.

Hebrews 12:22:

But ye are come unto mount Sion, and unto the city of the living God, the heavenly JERUSALEM, and to an innumerable company of angels,

Hebrews 13:14:

For here have we no continuing city, but we seek one to come.

Revelation 3:12:

Him that overcometh will I make a pillar in the temple of my God, and he shall go no more out: and I will write upon him the name of my God, and the name of the city of my God, which is new JERUSALEM, which cometh down out of heaven from my God: and I will write upon him my new name.

Revelation 21:2 & 10:

And I John saw the holy city, new JERUSALEM, coming down from God out of heaven, prepared as a bride adorned for her husband.

And he carried me away in the spirit to a great and high mountain, and shewed me that great city, the holy JERUSALEM, descending out of heaven from God,

Other Significant
Verses About *JERUSALEM*:

2 Chronicles 36:22-23:

Now in the first year of Cyrus king of Persia, that the word of the Lord spoken by the mouth of Jeremiah might be accomplished, the Lord stirred up the spirit of Cyrus king of Persia, that he made a proclamation throughout all his kingdom, and put it also in writing, saying,

Thus saith Cyrus king of Persia, All the kingdoms of the earth hath the Lord God of heaven given me; and he hath charged me to build him an house in JERUSALEM, which is in Judah. Who is there among you of all his people? The Lord his God be with him, and let him go up.

Psalms 51:18:

Do good in thy good pleasure unto Zion: build thou the walls of JERUSALEM.

Psalms 128:5:

The Lord shall bless thee out of Zion: and thou shalt see the good of JERUSALEM all the days of thy life.

Psalms 147:12-14:

Praise the Lord, O JERUSALEM; praise thy God, O Zion.

For he hath strengthened the bars of thy gates; he hath blessed thy children within thee.

He maketh peace in thy borders, and filleth thee with the finest of the wheat.

Isaiah 22:21-25:

And I will clothe him with thy robe, and strengthen him with thy girdle, and I will commit thy government into his hand: and he shall be a father to the inhabitants of JERUSALEM, and to the house of Judah.

And the key of the house of David will I lay upon his shoulder; so he shall open, and none shall shut; and he shall shut, and none shall open.

And I will fasten him as a nail in a sure place; and he shall be for a glorious throne to his father's house.

And they shall hang upon him all the glory of his father's house, the offspring and the issue, all vessels of small quantity, from the vessels of cups, even to all the vessels of flagons.

In that day, saith the Lord of hosts, shall the nail that is fastened in the sure place be removed, and be cut down, and fall; and the burden that was upon it shall be cut off: for the Lord hath spoken it.

Isaiah 40:2:

Speak ye comfortably to JERUSALEM, and cry unto her, that her warfare is accomplished, that her iniquity is pardoned: for she hath received of the Lord's hand double for all her sins.

Isaiah 41:27:

The first shall say to Zion, Behold, behold them: and I will give to JERUSALEM one that bringeth good tidings.

Isaiah 44:26-28:

That confirmeth the word of his servant, and performeth the counsel of his messengers; that saith to JERUSALEM, Thou shalt be inhabited; and to the cities of Judah, Ye shall be built, and I will raise up the decayed places thereof:

That saith to the deep, Be dry, and I will dry up thy rivers:

That saith of Cyrus, He is my shepherd, and shall perform all my pleasure: even saying to JERUSALEM, Thou shalt be built; and to the temple, Thy foundation shall be laid.

Isaiah 51:17:

Awake, awake, stand up, O JERUSALEM, which hast drunk at the hand of the Lord the cup of his fury; thou hast drunken the dregs of the cup of trembling, and wrung them out.

Isaiah 52:1-4:

Awake, awake; put on thy strength, O Zion; put on thy beautiful garments, O JERUSALEM, the holy city: for henceforth there shall no more come into thee the uncircumcised and the unclean.

Shake thyself from the dust; arise, and sit down, O JERUSALEM: loose thyself from the bands of thy neck, O captive daughter of Zion.

For thus saith the Lord, Ye have sold yourselves for nought; and ye shall be redeemed without money.

For thus saith the Lord God, My people went down aforetime into Egypt to sojourn there; and the Assyrian oppressed them without cause.

Isaiah 62:6-7:

I have set watchmen upon thy walls, O JERUSALEM, which shall never hold their peace day nor night: ye that make mention of the Lord, keep not silence,

And give him no rest, till he establish, and till he make JERUSALEM a praise in the earth.

Isaiah 65:18-19:

But be ye glad and rejoice for ever in that which I create: for, behold, I create JERUSALEM a rejoicing, and her people a joy.

And I will rejoice in JERUSALEM, and joy in my people: and the voice of weeping shall be no more heard in her, nor the voice of crying.

Isaiah 66:10:

Rejoice ye with JERUSALEM, and be glad with her, all ye that love her: rejoice for joy with her, all ye that mourn for her:

Jeremiah 2:2:

Go and cry in the ears of JERUSALEM, saying, Thus saith the Lord; I remember thee, the kindness of thy youth, the love of thine espousals, when thou wentest after me in the wilderness, in a land that was not sown.

Jeremiah 4:3-4:

For thus saith the Lord to the men of Judah and JERUSA-LEM, Break up your fallow ground, and sow not among thorns.

Circumcise yourselves to the Lord, and take away the foreskins of your heart, ye men of Judah and inhabitants of JERUSALEM:

Jeremiah 4:14:

O JERUSALEM, wash thine heart from wickedness, that thou mayest be saved. How long shall thy vain thoughts lodge within thee?

Jeremiah 5:1:

Run ye to and fro through the streets of JERUSALEM, and see now, and know, and seek in the broad places thereof, if ye can find a man, if there be any that executeth judgment, that seeketh the truth; and I will pardon it.

Jeremiah 6:8:

Be thou instructed, O JERUSALEM, lest my soul depart from thee; lest I make thee desolate, a land not inhabited.

Jeremiah 11:6:

Then the Lord said unto me, Proclaim all these words in the cities of Judah, and in the streets of JERUSALEM, saying, Hear ye the words of this covenant, and do them.

Jeremiah 15:5:

For who shall have pity upon thee, O JERUSALEM? or

who shall bemoan thee? or who shall go aside to ask how thou doest?

Jeremiah 17:26:

And they shall come from the cities of Judah, and from the places about JERUSALEM, and from the land of Benjamin, and from the plain, and from the mountains, and from the south, bringing burnt offerings, and sacrifices, and meat offerings, and incense, and bringing sacrifices of praise, unto the house of the Lord.

Jeremiah 27:18:

But if they be prophets, and if the word of the Lord be with them, let them now make intercession to the Lord of hosts, that the vessels which are left in the house of the Lord, and in the house of the king of Judah, and at JERUSALEM, go not to Babylon.

Jeremiah 34:8:

This is the word that came unto Jeremiah from the Lord, after that the king Zedekiah had made a covenant with all the people which were at JERUSALEM, to proclaim liberty unto them;

Jeremiah 51:50:

Ye that have escaped the sword, go away, stand not still: remember the Lord afar off, and let JERUSALEM come into your mind.

Ezekiel 8:3:

And he put forth the form of an hand, and took me by a

lock of mine head; and the spirit lifted me up between the earth and the heaven, and brought me in the visions of God to JERUSALEM, to the door of the inner gate that looketh toward the north; where was the seat of the image of jealousy, which provoketh to jealousy.

Ezekiel 9:4:

And the Lord said unto him, Go through the midst of the city, through the midst of JERUSALEM, and set a mark upon the foreheads of the men that sigh and that cry for all the abominations that be done in the midst thereof.

Zephaniah 1:12:

And it shall come to pass at that time, that I will search JERUSALEM with candles, and punish the men that are settled on their lees: that say in their heart, The Lord will not do good, neither will he do evil.

Zechariah 3:2:

And the Lord said unto Satan, The Lord rebuke thee, O Satan; even the Lord that hath chosen JERUSALEM rebuke thee: is not this a brand plucked out of the fire?

Zechariah 7:7:

Should ye not hear the words which the Lord hath cried by the former prophets, when JERUSALEM was inhabited and in prosperity, and the cities thereof round about her, when men inhabited the south and the plain?

Zechariah 12:6-8:

And JERUSALEM shall be inhabited again in her own place, even in JERUSALEM.

The Lord also shall save the tents of Judah first, that the glory of the house of David and the glory of the inhabitants of JERUSALEM do not magnify themselves against Judah.

In that day shall the Lord defend the inhabitants of JERUSALEM; and he that is feeble among them at that day shall be as David; and the house of David shall be as God, as the angel of the Lord before them.

Zechariah 12:9-11:

And it shall come to pass in that day, that I will seek to destroy all the nations that come against JERUSALEM.

And I will pour upon the house of David, and upon the inhabitants of JERUSALEM, the spirit of grace and of supplications: and they shall look upon me whom they have pierced, and they shall mourn for him, as one mourneth for his only son, and shall be in bitterness for him, as one that is in bitterness for his firstborn.

In that day shall there be a great mourning in JERUSALEM, as the mourning of Hadadrimmon in the valley of Megiddon.

Matthew 23:37-39:

O JERUSALEM, JERUSALEM, thou that killest the prophets, and stonest them which are sent unto thee, how often would I have gathered thy children together, even as a hen gathereth her chickens under her wings, and ye would not!

Behold, your house is left unto you desolate.

For I say unto you, Ye shall not see me henceforth, till ye shall say, Blessed is he that cometh in the name of the Lord.

Zion

Psalms 87:1-7:

His foundation is in the holy mountains.

The Lord loveth the gates of ZION more than all the dwellings of Jacob.

Glorious things are spoken of thee, O city of God. Selah.

I will make mention of Rahab and Babylon to them that know me: behold Philistia, and Tyre, with Ethiopia; this man was born there.

And of ZION it shall be said, This and that man was born in her: and the highest himself shall establish her.

The Lord shall count, when he writeth up the people, that this man was born there. Selah.

As well the singers as the players on instruments shall be there: all my springs are in thee.

ZION Past

(ZION is a very broad term. It can refer to the city of Jerusalem, to the whole of Israel, to the people of God, to the Kingdom of God, or to the Temple, as a focal point.)

ZION: The Name of the Stronghold Captured by David From the Jebusites.

2 Samuel 5:6-9:

And the king and his men went to Jerusalem unto the Jebusites, the inhabitants of the land: which spake unto David, saying, Except thou take away the blind and the lame, thou shalt not come in hither: thinking, David cannot come in hither.

Nevertheless David took the strong hold of ZION: the same is the city of David.

And David said on that day, Whosoever getteth up to the gutter, and smiteth the Jebusites, and the lame and the blind that are hated of David's soul, he shall be chief and captain. Wherefore they said, The blind and the lame shall not come into the house.

So David dwelt in the fort, and called it the city of David. And David built round about from Millo and inward.

1 Chronicles 11:5-7:
And the inhabitants of Jebus said to David, Thou shalt not come hither. Nevertheless David took the castle of ZION, which is the city of David.

And David said, Whosoever smiteth the Jebusites first shall be chief and captain. So Joab the son of Zeruiah went first up, and was chief.

And David dwelt in the castle; therefore they called it the city of David.

ZION Came to Be Called "The City of David."

1 Kings 8:1:
Then Solomon assembled the elders of Israel, and all the heads of the tribes, the chief of the fathers of the children of Israel, unto king Solomon in Jerusalem, that they might bring up the ark of the covenant of the Lord out of **the city of David**, which is ZION.

ZION: The Place to Which David Brought the Ark of the Covenant.

1 Chronicles 15:1:
And David made him houses in the city of David, and prepared a place for the ark of God, and pitched for it a tent.

1 Chronicles 15:29:
And it came to pass, as the ark of the covenant of the

Lord came to the city of David, that Michal, the daughter of Saul looking out at a window saw king David dancing and playing: and she despised him in her heart.

2 *Chronicles 5:2:*

Then Solomon assembled the elders of Israel, and all the heads of the tribes, the chief of the fathers of the children of Israel, unto Jerusalem, to bring up the ark of the covenant of the Lord out of the city of David, which is ZION.

ZION: The Name Transferred to Mt. Moriah When Solomon Built the Temple There and When the Ark Was Moved There

2 *Chronicles 3:1:*

Then Solomon began to build the house of the Lord at Jerusalem in mount Moriah, where the Lord appeared unto David his father, in the place that David had prepared in the threshingfloor of Ornan the Jebusite.

ZION: The Most Significant of All Sacred Places to the Prophets and the People of God

Jeremiah 31:6:

For there shall be a day, that the watchmen upon the mount Ephraim shall cry, Arise ye, and let us go up to ZION unto the Lord our God.

Zechariah 8:2-3:

Thus saith the Lord of hosts; I was jealous for ZION with great jealousy, and I was jealous for her with great fury.

Thus saith the Lord; I am returned unto ZION, and will dwell in the midst of Jerusalem: and Jerusalem shall be called a city of truth; and the mountain of the Lord of hosts the holy mountain.

ZION: A Name Used For the Whole of Jerusalem, at Times

Psalms 87:2:

The Lord loveth the gates of ZION more than all the dwellings of Jacob.

Psalms 87:5:

And of ZION it shall be said, This and that man was born in her: and the highest himself shall establish her.

Psalms 149:2:

Let Israel rejoice in him that made him: let the children of ZION be joyful in their King.

Song of Songs 3:11:

Go forth, O ye daughters of ZION, and behold king Solomon with the crown wherewith his mother crowned him in the day of his espousals, and in the day of the gladness of his heart.

Isaiah 33:14:

The sinners in ZION are afraid; fearfulness hath surprised the hypocrites. Who among us shall dwell with the devouring fire? who among us shall dwell with everlasting burnings?

Isaiah 33:20:

Look upon ZION, the city of our solemnities: thine eyes shall see Jerusalem a quiet habitation, a tabernacle that shall not be taken down; not one of the stakes thereof shall ever be removed, neither shall any of the cords thereof be broken.

Jeremiah 9:19:

For a voice of wailing is heard out of ZION, How are we spoiled! we are greatly confounded, because we have forsaken the land, because our dwellings have cast us out.

Jeremiah 30:17:

For I will restore health unto thee, and I will heal thee of thy wounds, saith the Lord; because they called thee an Outcast, saying, This is ZION, whom no man seeketh after.

ZION: As A People

Psalms 78:68:

But chose the tribe of Judah, the MOUNT ZION which he loved.

ZION Present and Future

ZION: Chosen of God to Bless the Nations

Isaiah 28:16:

Therefore thus saith the Lord God, Behold, I lay in ZION for a foundation a stone, a tried stone, a precious corner stone, a sure foundation: he that believeth shall not make haste.

Romans 9:33:

As it is written, Behold, I lay in SION a stumblingstone and rock of offence: and whosoever believeth on him shall not be ashamed.

Psalms 2:6:

Yet have I set my king upon my holy hill of ZION.

Psalms 9:11:

Sing praises to the Lord, which dwelleth in ZION: declare among the people his doings.

Psalms 20:2:

Send thee help from the sanctuary, and strengthen thee out of ZION;

Psalms 50:2:

Out of ZION, the perfection of beauty, God hath shined.

Psalms 76:2:

In Salem also is his tabernacle, and his dwelling place in ZION.

Psalms 128:5:

The Lord shall bless thee out of ZION: and thou shalt see the good of Jerusalem all the days of thy life.

Psalms 132:13-14:

For the Lord hath chosen ZION; he hath desired it for his habitation.

This is my rest for ever: here will I dwell; for I have desired it.

Psalms 135:21:

Blessed be the Lord out of ZION, which dwelleth at Jerusalem. Praise ye the Lord.

Psalms 146:10:

The Lord shall reign for ever, even thy God, O ZION, unto all generations. Praise ye the Lord.

Isaiah 2:3:

And many people shall go and say, Come ye, and let us

go up to the mountain of the Lord, to the house of the God of Jacob; and he will teach us of his ways, and we will walk in his paths: for out of ZION shall go forth the law, and the word of the Lord from Jerusalem.

Isaiah 30:19:

For the people shall dwell in ZION at Jerusalem: thou shalt weep no more: he will be very gracious unto thee at the voice of thy cry; when he shall hear it, he will answer thee.

Look upon Zion, the city of our solemnities: thine eyes shall see Jerusalem a quiet habitation, a tabernacle that shall not be taken down; not one of the stakes thereof shall ever be removed, neither shall any of the cords thereof be broken.

But there the glorious Lord will be unto us a place of broad rivers and streams; wherein shall go no galley with oars, neither shall gallant ship pass thereby.

Isaiah 35:10:

And the ransomed of the Lord shall return, and come to ZION with songs and everlasting joy upon their heads: they shall obtain joy and gladness, and sorrow and sighing shall flee away.

Isaiah 46:13:

I bring near my righteousness; it shall not be far off, and my salvation shall not tarry: and I will place salvation in ZION for Israel my glory.

Isaiah 51:3:

For the Lord shall comfort ZION: he will comfort all her

waste places; and he will make her wilderness like Eden, and her desert like the garden of the Lord; joy and gladness shall be found therein, thanksgiving, and the voice of melody.

Isaiah 52:7-8:

How beautiful upon the mountains are the feet of him that bringeth good tidings, that publisheth peace; that bringeth good tidings of good, that publisheth salvation; that saith unto ZION, Thy God reigneth!

Thy watchmen shall lift up the voice; with the voice together shall they sing: for they shall see eye to eye, when the Lord shall bring again ZION.

Isaiah 59:20:

And the Redeemer shall come to ZION, and unto them that turn from transgression in Jacob, saith the Lord.

Joel 2:22-23:

Be not afraid, ye beasts of the field: for the pastures of the wilderness do spring, for the tree beareth her fruit, the fig tree and the vine do yield their strength.

Be glad then, ye children of ZION, and rejoice in the Lord your God: for he hath given you the former rain moderately, and he will cause to come down for you the rain, the former rain, and the latter rain in the first month

Joel 3:16-17:

The Lord also shall roar out of ZION, and utter his voice from Jerusalem; and the heavens and the earth shall shake: but the Lord will be the hope of his people, and the strength of the children of Israel.

So shall ye know that I am the Lord your God dwelling in ZION, my holy mountain: then shall Jerusalem be holy, and there shall no strangers pass through her any more.

Micah 4:2:

And many nations shall come, and say, Come, and let us go up to the mountain of the Lord, and to the house of the God of Jacob; and he will teach us of his ways, and we will walk in his paths: for the law shall go forth of ZION, and the word of the Lord from Jerusalem.

Zechariah 2:6-9:

Ho, Ho, come forth, and flee from the land of the north, saith the Lord: for I have spread you abroad as the four winds of the heaven, saith the Lord.

Deliver thyself, O ZION, that dwellest with the daughter of Babylon.

For thus saith the Lord of hosts; After the glory hath he sent me unto the nations which spoiled you: for he that toucheth you toucheth the apple of his eye.

For, behold, I will shake mine hand upon them, and they shall be a spoil to their servants: and ye shall know that the Lord of hosts hath sent me.

ZION: The Place From Which the Deliverer Will Come Forth

Romans 11:26:

And so all Israel shall be saved: as it is written, There shall come out of SION the Deliverer, and shall turn away ungodliness from Jacob:

ZION: Her Restoration

According to the Psalmist:

Psalms 69:35-36:

For God will save ZION, and will build the cities of Judah: that they may dwell there, and have it in possession.

The seed also of his servants shall inherit it: and they that love his name shall dwell therein.

Psalms 102:13-16:

Thou shalt arise, and have mercy upon ZION: for the time to favour her, yea, the set time, is come.

For thy servants take pleasure in her stones, and favour the dust thereof.

So the heathen shall fear the name of the Lord, and all the kings of the earth thy glory.

When the Lord shall build up ZION, he shall appear in his glory.

Psalms 126:1-6:

When the Lord turned again the captivity of ZION, we were like them that dream.

Then was our mouth filled with laughter, and our tongue with singing: then said they among the heathen, The Lord hath done great things for them.

The Lord hath done great things for us; whereof we are glad.

Turn again our captivity, O Lord, as the streams in the south.

They that sow in tears shall reap in joy.

He that goeth forth and weepeth, bearing precious seed, shall doubtless come again with rejoicing, bringing his sheaves with him.

According to Isaiah:

Isaiah 51:3:
For the Lord shall comfort ZION: he will comfort all her waste places; and he will make her wilderness like Eden, and her desert like the garden of the Lord; joy and gladness shall be found therein, thanksgiving, and the voice of melody.

Isaiah 51:11:
Therefore the redeemed of the Lord shall return, and come with singing unto ZION; and everlasting joy shall be upon their head: they shall obtain gladness and joy; and sorrow and mourning shall flee away.

Isaiah 51:16:
And I have put my words in thy mouth, and I have covered thee in the shadow of mine hand, that I may plant the heavens, and lay the foundations of the earth, and say unto ZION, Thou art my people.

Isaiah 52:1-2:
Awake, awake; put on thy strength, O ZION; put on thy beautiful garments, O Jerusalem, the holy city: for henceforth there shall no more come into thee the uncircumcised and the unclean.

Shake thyself from the dust; arise, and sit down, O Jerusalem: loose thyself from the bands of thy neck, O captive daughter of ZION.

Isaiah 52:7-8:

How beautiful upon the mountains are the feet of him that bringeth good tidings, that publisheth peace; that bringeth good tidings of good, that publisheth salvation; that saith unto ZION, Thy God reigneth!

Thy watchmen shall lift up the voice; with the voice together shall they sing: for they shall see eye to eye, when the Lord shall bring again ZION.

Isaiah 60:14:

The sons also of them that afflicted thee shall come bending unto thee; and all they that despised thee shall bow themselves down at the soles of thy feet; and they shall call thee; The city of the Lord, The ZION of the Holy One of Israel.

According to Zephaniah:

Zephaniah 3:14-16:

Sing, O daughter of ZION; shout, O Israel; be glad and rejoice with all the heart, O daughter of Jerusalem.

The Lord hath taken away thy judgments, he hath cast out thine enemy: the king of Israel, even the Lord, is in the midst of thee: thou shalt not see evil any more.

In that day it shall be said to Jerusalem, Fear thou not: and to ZION, Let not thine hands be slack.

According to Zechariah:

Zechariah 1:14:
So the angel that communed with me said unto me, Cry thou, saying, Thus saith the Lord of hosts; I am jealous for Jerusalem and for ZION with a great jealousy.

Zechariah 1:17:
Cry yet, saying, Thus saith the Lord of hosts; My cities through prosperity shall yet be spread abroad; and the Lord shall yet comfort ZION, and shall yet choose Jerusalem.

Zechariah 2:7:
Deliver thyself, O ZION, that dwellest with the daughter of Babylon.

Zechariah 2:10:
Sing and rejoice, O daughter of ZION: for, lo, I come, and I will dwell in the midst of thee, saith the Lord.

Zechariah 8:3:
Thus saith the Lord; I am returned unto ZION, and will dwell in the midst of Jerusalem: and Jerusalem shall be called a city of truth; and the mountain of the Lord of hosts the holy mountain.

Zechariah 9:9:
Rejoice greatly, O daughter of ZION; shout, O daughter of Jerusalem: behold, thy King cometh unto thee: he is just, and having salvation; lowly, and riding upon an ass, and upon a colt the foal of an ass.

MOUNT ZION

2 Kings 19:31:

For out of Jerusalem shall go forth a remnant, and they that escape out of MOUNT ZION: the zeal of the Lord of hosts shall do this.

Psalms 48:2-3:

Beautiful for situation, the joy of the whole earth, is MOUNT ZION, on the sides of the north, the city of the great King.

God is known in her palaces for a refuge.

Psalms 48:11:

Let MOUNT ZION rejoice, let the daughters of Judah be glad, because of thy judgments.

Psalms 74:2:

Remember thy congregation, which thou hast purchased of old; the rod of thine inheritance, which thou hast redeemed; this MOUNT ZION, wherein thou hast dwelt.

Psalms 78:68:

But chose the tribe of Judah, the MOUNT ZION which he loved.

Psalms 125:1-2:

They that trust in the Lord shall be as MOUNT ZION, which cannot be removed, but abideth for ever.

As the mountains are round about Jerusalem, so the Lord is round about his people from henceforth even for ever.

Isaiah 4:5:

And the Lord will create upon every dwelling place of MOUNT ZION, and upon her assemblies, a cloud and smoke by day, and the shining of a flaming fire by night: for upon all the glory shall be a defence.

Isaiah 8:18:

Behold, I and the children whom the Lord hath given me are for signs and for wonders in Israel from the Lord of hosts, which dwelleth in MOUNT ZION.

Isaiah 10:12:

Wherefore it shall come to pass, that when the Lord hath performed his whole work upon MOUNT ZION and on Jerusalem, I will punish the fruit of the stout heart of the king of Assyria, and the glory of his high looks.

Isaiah 24:23:

Then the moon shall be confounded, and the sun ashamed,

when the Lord of hosts shall reign in MOUNT ZION, and in Jerusalem, and before his ancients gloriously.

Isaiah 29:7-8:

And the multitude of all the nations that fight against Ariel, even all that fight against her and her munition, and that distress her, shall be as a dream of a night vision.

It shall even be as when an hungry man dreameth, and, behold, he eateth; but he awaketh, and his soul is empty: or as when a thirsty man dreameth, and, behold, he drinketh; but he awaketh, and, behold, he is faint, and his soul hath appetite: so shall the multitude of all the nations be, that fight against mount ZION.

Isaiah 31:4-5 & 9:

For thus hath the Lord spoken unto me, Like as the lion and the young lion roaring on his prey, when a multitude of shepherds is called forth against him, he will not be afraid of their voice, nor abase himself for the noise of them: so shall the Lord of hosts come down to fight for MOUNT ZION, and for the hill thereof.

As birds flying, so will the Lord of hosts defend Jerusalem; defending also he will deliver it; and passing over he will preserve it.

... saith the Lord, whose fire is in ZION, and his furnace in Jerusalem.

Isaiah 37:32:

For out of Jerusalem shall go forth a remnant, and they that escape out of MOUNT ZION: the zeal of the Lord of hosts shall do this.

Joel 2:32:

And it shall come to pass, that whosoever shall call on the name of the Lord shall be delivered: for in MOUNT ZION and in Jerusalem shall be deliverance, as the Lord hath said, and in the remnant whom the Lord shall call.

Obadiah 1:17 & 21:

But upon MOUNT ZION shall be deliverance, and there shall be holiness; and the house of Jacob shall possess their possessions.

And saviours shall come up on MOUNT ZION to judge the mount of Esau; and the kingdom shall be the Lord's.

Micah 4:7:

And I will make her that halted a remnant, and her that was cast far off a strong nation: and the Lord shall reign over them in MOUNT ZION from henceforth, even for ever.

Hebrews 12:22:

But ye are come unto MOUNT SION, and unto the city of the living God, the heavenly Jerusalem, and to an innumerable company of angels,

Revelation 14:1:

And I looked, and, lo, a Lamb stood on the MOUNT SION, and with him an hundred forty and four thousand, having his Father's name written in their foreheads.

ZION: The Mountain of the Lord

Psalms 15:1:

Lord, who shall abide in thy tabernacle? who shall dwell in thy holy hill?

Exodus 15:17-18:

Thou shalt bring them in, and plant them in the MOUN-TAIN of thine inheritance, in the place, O Lord, which thou hast made for thee to dwell in, in the Sanctuary, O Lord, which thy hands have established.

The Lord shall reign for ever and ever.

Psalms 48:1:

Great is the Lord, and greatly to be praised in the city of our God, in the MOUNTAIN of his holiness.

Psalms 87:1:

His foundation is in the holy MOUNTAINS.

Psalms 133:3:

As the dew of Hermon, and as the dew that descended

upon the MOUNTAINS of ZION: for there the Lord commanded the blessing, even life for evermore.

Isaiah 2:2:

And it shall come to pass in the last days, that the MOUNTAIN of the Lord's house shall be established in the top of the MOUNTAINS, and shall be exalted above the hills; and all nations shall flow unto it.

Isaiah 2:3:

And many people shall go and say, Come ye, and let us go up to the MOUNTAIN of the Lord, to the house of the God of Jacob; and he will teach us of his ways, and we will walk in his paths: for out of ZION shall go forth the law, and the word of the Lord from Jerusalem.

Isaiah 11:9:

They shall not hurt nor destroy in all my holy MOUNTAIN: for the earth shall be full of the knowledge of the Lord, as the waters cover the sea.

Isaiah 25:6:

And in this MOUNTAIN shall the Lord of hosts make unto all people a feast of fat things, a feast of wines on the lees, of fat things full of marrow, of wines on the lees well refined.

Isaiah 25:7:

And he will destroy in this MOUNTAIN the face of the

covering cast over all people, and the vail that is spread over all nations.

Isaiah 25:10:

For in this MOUNTAIN shall the hand of the Lord rest, and Moab shall be trodden down under him, even as straw is trodden down for the dunghill.

Isaiah 30:29:

Ye shall have a song, as in the night when a holy solemnity is kept; and gladness of heart, as when one goeth with a pipe to come into the MOUNTAIN of the Lord, to the mighty One of Israel.

Isaiah 40:9:

O ZION, that bringest good tidings, get thee up into the high MOUNTAIN; O Jerusalem, that bringest good tidings, lift up thy voice with strength; lift it up, be not afraid; say unto the cities of Judah, Behold your God!

Isaiah 56:7:

Even them will I bring to my holy MOUNTAIN, and make them joyful in my house of prayer: their burnt offerings and their sacrifices shall be accepted upon mine altar; for mine house shall be called an house of prayer for all people.

Isaiah 57:13:

When thou criest, let thy companies deliver thee; but the wind shall carry them all away; vanity shall take them: but he that putteth his trust in me shall possess the land, and shall inherit my holy MOUNTAIN;

Isaiah 65:25:

The wolf and the lamb shall feed together, and the lion shall eat straw like the bullock: and dust shall be the serpent's meat. They shall not hurt nor destroy in all my holy MOUNTAIN, saith the Lord.

Isaiah 66:20:

And they shall bring all your brethren for an offering unto the Lord out of all nations upon horses, and in chariots, and in litters, and upon mules, and upon swift beasts, to my holy MOUNTAIN Jerusalem, saith the Lord, as the children of Israel bring an offering in a clean vessel into the house of the Lord.

Jeremiah 31:23:

Thus saith the Lord of hosts, the God of Israel; As yet they shall use this speech in the land of Judah and in the cities thereof, when I shall bring again their captivity; the Lord bless thee, O habitation of justice, and MOUNTAIN of holiness.

Ezekiel 17:22:

Thus saith the Lord God; I will also take of the highest branch of the high cedar, and will set it; I will crop off from the top of his young twigs a tender one, and will plant it upon an high MOUNTAIN and eminent:

Ezekiel 17:23:

In the MOUNTAIN of the height of Israel will I plant it:

and it shall bring forth boughs, and bear fruit, and be a goodly cedar: and under it shall dwell all fowl of every wing; in the shadow of the branches thereof shall they dwell.

Ezekiel 20:40:

For in mine holy MOUNTAIN, in the MOUNTAIN of the height of Israel, saith the Lord God, there shall all the house of Israel, all of them in the land, serve me: there will I accept them, and there will I require your offerings, and the firstfruits of your oblations, with all your holy things.

Ezekiel 43:12:

This is the law of the house; Upon the top of the MOUNTAIN the whole limit thereof round about shall be most holy. Behold, this is the law of the house.

Daniel 9:16:

O Lord, according to all thy righteousness, I beseech thee, let thine anger and thy fury be turned away from thy city Jerusalem, thy holy MOUNTAIN: because for our sins, and for the iniquities of our fathers, Jerusalem and thy people are become a reproach to all that are about us.

Daniel 9:20-21:

And whiles I was speaking, and praying, and confessing my sin and the sin of my people Israel, and presenting my supplication before the Lord my God for the holy MOUNTAIN of my God;

Yea, whiles I was speaking in prayer, even the man Gabriel, whom I had seen in the vision at the beginning, being caused to fly swiftly, touched me about the time of the evening oblation.

Joel 2:1:

Blow ye the trumpet in ZION, and sound an alarm in my holy MOUNTAIN: let all the inhabitants of the land tremble: for the day of the Lord cometh, for it is nigh at hand;

Joel 3:17-18:

So shall ye know that I am the Lord your God dwelling in ZION, my holy MOUNTAIN: then shall Jerusalem be holy, and there shall no strangers pass through her any more.

And it shall come to pass in that day, that the MOUNTAINS shall drop down new wine, and the hills shall flow with milk, and all the rivers of Judah shall flow with waters, and a fountain shall come forth of the house of the Lord, and shall water the valley of Shittim.

Obadiah 1:16:

For as ye have drunk upon my holy MOUNTAIN, so shall all the heathen drink continually, yea, they shall drink, and they shall swallow down, and they shall be as though they had not been.

Micah 4:1:

But in the last days it shall come to pass, that the MOUNTAIN of the house of the Lord shall be established in the top of the MOUNTAINS, and it shall be exalted above the hills; and people shall flow unto it.

Micah 4:2:

And many nations shall come, and say, Come, and let us go up to the MOUNTAIN of the Lord, and to the house of the God of Jacob; and he will teach us of his ways, and we will walk in his paths: for the law shall go forth of ZION, and the word of the Lord from Jerusalem.

Zephaniah 3:11:

In that day shalt thou not be ashamed for all thy doings, wherein thou hast transgressed against me: for then I will take away out of the midst of thee them that rejoice in thy pride, and thou shalt no more be haughty because of my holy MOUNTAIN.

Haggai 1:8:

Go up to the MOUNTAIN, and bring wood, and build the house; and I will take pleasure in it, and I will be glorified, saith the Lord.

Zechariah 8:3:

Thus saith the Lord; I am returned unto ZION, and will dwell in the midst of Jerusalem: and Jerusalem shall be called a city of truth; and the MOUNTAIN of the Lord of hosts the holy MOUNTAIN.

Other Significant Verses About ZION

Psalms 48:12:
Walk about ZION, and go round about her: tell the towers thereof.

Psalms 51:18:
Do good in thy good pleasure unto ZION: build thou the walls of Jerusalem.

Psalms 97:8:
ZION heard, and was glad; and the daughters of Judah rejoiced because of thy judgments, O Lord.

Psalms 99:2:
The Lord is great in ZION; and he is high above all the people.

Psalms 102:16:
When the Lord shall build up ZION, he shall appear in his glory.

Psalms 102:21:

To declare the name of the Lord in ZION, and his praise in Jerusalem;

Psalms 110:2-3:

The Lord shall send the rod of thy strength out of ZION: rule thou in the midst of thine enemies.

Thy people shall be willing in the day of thy power, in the beauties of holiness from the womb of the morning: thou hast the dew of thy youth.

Psalms 128:5:

The Lord shall bless thee out of ZION: and thou shalt see the good of Jerusalem all the days of thy life.

Psalms 137:1-4:

By the rivers of Babylon, there we sat down, yea, we wept, when we remembered ZION.

We hanged our harps upon the willows in the midst thereof.

For there they that carried us away captive required of us a song; and they that wasted us required of us mirth, saying, Sing us one of the songs of ZION.

How shall we sing the Lord's song in a strange land?

Psalms 147:12-14:

Praise the Lord, O Jerusalem; praise thy God, O ZION.

For he hath strengthened the bars of thy gates; he hath blessed thy children within thee.

He maketh peace in thy borders, and filleth thee with the finest of the wheat.

Isaiah 14:32:
What shall one then answer the messengers of the nation? That the Lord hath founded ZION, and the poor of his people shall trust in it.

Isaiah 41:27:
The first shall say to ZION, Behold, behold them: and I will give to Jerusalem one that bringeth good tidings.

Isaiah 49:14-16:
But ZION said, The Lord hath forsaken me, and my Lord hath forgotten me.

Can a woman forget her sucking child, that she should not have compassion on the son of her womb? yea, they may forget, yet will I not forget thee.

Behold, I have graven thee upon the palms of my hands; thy walls are continually before me.

Lamentations 1:17:
ZION spreadeth forth her hands, and there is none to comfort her:

Lamentations 2:13:
What thing shall I take to witness for thee? what thing shall I liken to thee, O daughter of Jerusalem? what shall I equal to thee, that I may comfort thee, O virgin daughter of ZION? for thy breach is great like the sea: who can heal thee?

Amos 1:2:

And he said, The Lord will roar from ZION, and utter his voice from Jerusalem; and the habitations of the shepherds shall mourn, and the top of Carmel shall wither.

Israel

Isaiah 44:1-8 & 21-28:

Yet now hear, O Jacob my servant; and ISRAEL, whom I have chosen:

Thus saith the Lord that made thee, and formed thee from the womb, which will help thee; Fear not, O Jacob, my servant; and thou, Jesurun, whom I have chosen.

For I will pour water upon him that is thirsty, and floods upon the dry ground: I will pour my spirit upon thy seed, and my blessing upon thine offspring:

And they shall spring up as among the grass, as willows by the water courses.

One shall say, I am the Lord's; and another shall call himself by the name of Jacob; and another shall subscribe with his hand unto the Lord, and surname himself by the name of ISRAEL.

Thus saith the Lord the King of ISRAEL, and his redeemer the Lord of hosts; I am the first, and I am the last; and beside me there is no God.

And who, as I, shall call, and shall declare it, and set it in order for me, since I appointed the ancient people? and the things that are coming, and shall come, let them shew unto them.

Fear ye not, neither be afraid: have not I told thee from that time, and have declared it? ye are even my witnesses. Is there a God beside me? yea, there is no God; I know not any.

Remember these, O Jacob and ISRAEL; for thou art my servant: I have formed thee; thou art my servant: O ISRAEL, thou shalt not be forgotten of me.

I have blotted out, as a thick cloud, thy transgressions, and, as a cloud, thy sins: return unto me; for I have redeemed thee.

Sing, O ye heavens; for the Lord hath done it: shout, ye lower parts of the earth: break forth into singing, ye mountains, O forest, and every tree therein: for the Lord hath redeemed Jacob, and glorified himself in ISRAEL.

Thus saith the Lord, thy redeemer, and he that formed thee from the womb, I am the Lord that maketh all things; that stretcheth forth the heavens alone; that spreadeth abroad the earth by myself;

That frustrateth the tokens of the liars, and maketh diviners mad; that turneth wise men backward, and maketh their knowledge foolish;

That confirmeth the word of his servant, and performeth the counsel of his messengers; that saith to Jerusalem, Thou shalt be inhabited; and to the cities of Judah, Ye shall be built, and I will raise up the decayed places thereof:

That saith to the deep, Be dry, and I will dry up thy rivers:

That saith of Cyrus, He is my shepherd, and shall perform all my pleasure: even saying to Jerusalem, Thou shalt be built; and to the temple, Thy foundation shall be laid.

ISRAEL:
The Land and Its Promises

ISRAEL: A Description of the Land

Genesis 13:10:

And Lot lifted up his eyes, and beheld all the plain of Jordan, that it was well watered every where, before the Lord destroyed Sodom and Gomorrah, even as the garden of the Lord, like the land of Egypt, as thou comest unto Zoar.

Exodus 3:8:

And I am come down to deliver them out of the hand of the Egyptians, and to bring them up out of that land unto a good land and a large, unto a land flowing with milk and honey; unto the place of the Canaanites, and the Hittites, and the Amorites, and the Perizzites, and the Hivites, and the Jebusites.

Numbers 13:27:

And they told him, and said, We came unto the land

whither thou sentest us, and surely it floweth with milk and honey; and this is the fruit of it.

Numbers 14:8:

If the Lord delight in us, then he will bring us into this land, and give it us; a land which floweth with milk and honey.

Deuteronomy 8:7-10:

For the Lord thy God bringeth thee into a good land, a land of brooks of water, of fountains and depths that spring out of valleys and hills;

A land of wheat, and barley, and vines, and fig trees, and pomegranates; a land of oil olive, and honey;

A land wherein thou shalt eat bread without scarceness, thou shalt not lack any thing in it; a land whose stones are iron, and out of whose hills thou mayest dig brass.

When thou hast eaten and art full, then thou shalt bless the Lord thy God for the good land which he hath given thee.

Deuteronomy 11:9-12:

And that ye may prolong your days in the land, which the Lord sware unto your fathers to give unto them and to their seed, a land that floweth with milk and honey.

For the land, whither thou goest in to possess it, is not as the land of Egypt, from whence ye came out, where thou sowedst thy seed, and wateredst it with thy foot, as a garden of herbs:

But the land, whither ye go to possess it, is a land of hills and valleys, and drinketh water of the rain of heaven:

A land which the Lord thy God careth for: the eyes of the

Lord thy God are always upon it, from the beginning of the year even unto the end of the year.

Jeremiah 2:7:

And I brought you into a plentiful country, to eat the fruit thereof and the goodness thereof;

ISRAEL: Names of the Land

Beulah

Isaiah 62:4:

Thou shalt no more be termed Forsaken; neither shall thy land any more be termed Desolate: but thou shalt be called Hephzibah, and thy land **Beulah**: for the Lord delighteth in thee, and thy land shall be married.

Canaan

Genesis 11:31:

And Terah took Abram his son, and Lot the son of Haran his son's son, and Sarai his daughter in law, his son Abram's wife; and they went forth with them from Ur of the Chaldees, to go into the land of **Canaan**; and they came unto Haran, and dwelt there.

Goodly Mountain

Deuteronomy 3:25:

I pray thee, let me go over, and see the good land that is beyond Jordan, **that goodly mountain**, and Lebanon.

Holy Land

Zechariah 2:12:

And the Lord shall inherit Judah his portion in **the holy land,** and shall choose Jerusalem again.

Immanuel's Land

Isaiah 8:8:

And he shall pass through Judah; he shall overflow and go over, he shall reach even to the neck; and the stretching out of his wings shall fill the breadth of thy land, O **Immanuel.**

Jeshurun

Deuteronomy 33:26:

There is none like unto the God of **Jeshurun,** who rideth upon the heaven in thy help, and in his excellency on the sky.

Isaiah 44:2:

Thus saith the Lord that made thee, and formed thee from the womb, which will help thee; Fear not, O Jacob, my servant; and thou, **Jesurun,** whom I have chosen.

Land of ISRAEL

1 Samuel 13:19:

Now there was no smith found throughout all the **land of ISRAEL:** for the Philistines said, Lest the Hebrews make them swords or spears:

Land of the Hebrews

Genesis 40:15:

For indeed I was stolen away out of **the land of the Hebrews**: and here also have I done nothing that they should put me into the dungeon.

Land of the Jews

Acts 10:39:

And we are witnesses of all things which he did both in **the land of the Jews**, and in Jerusalem;

Land of Promise

Hebrews 11:9:

By faith he sojourned in **the land of promise**, as in a strange country, dwelling in tabernacles with Isaac and Jacob, the heirs with him of the same promise:

Palestina

Exodus 15:14:

The people shall hear, And be afraid: sorrow shall take hold on the inhabitants of **Palestina.**

Pleasant Land

Daniel 8:9:

And out of one of them came forth a little horn, which

waxed exceeding great, toward the south, and toward the east, and toward **the pleasant land.**

Zechariah 7:14:
But I scattered them with a whirlwind among all the nations whom they knew not. Thus the land was desolate after them, that no man passed through nor returned: for they laid **the pleasant land** desolate.

The Lord's Land

Hosea 9:3:
They shall not dwell in **the Lord's land;** but Ephraim shall return to Egypt, and they shall eat unclean things in Assyria.

ISRAEL: A Land Promised to Abraham and His Descendants

Genesis 12:7:
And the Lord appeared unto Abram, and said, Unto thy seed will I give this land: and there builded he an altar unto the Lord, who appeared unto him.

Genesis 13:15:
For all the land which thou seest, to thee will I give it, and to thy seed for ever.

Genesis 15:7:
And he said unto him, I am the Lord that brought thee out of Ur of the Chaldees, to give thee this land to inherit it.

Genesis 15:18:

In the same day the Lord made a covenant with Abram, saying, Unto thy seed have I given this land, from the river of Egypt unto the great river, the river Euphrates:

Genesis 17:8:

And I will give unto thee, and to thy seed after thee, the land wherein thou art a stranger, all the land of Canaan, for an everlasting possession; and I will be their God.

Genesis 50:24:

And Joseph said unto his brethren, I die: and God will surely visit you, and bring you out of this land unto the land which he sware to Abraham, to Isaac, and to Jacob.

Exodus 6:8:

And I will bring you in unto the land, concerning the which I did swear to give it to Abraham, to Isaac, and to Jacob; and I will give it you for an heritage: I am the Lord.

Deuteronomy 6:10:

And it shall be, when the Lord thy God shall have brought thee into the land which he sware unto thy fathers, to Abraham, to Isaac, and to Jacob, to give thee great and goodly cities, which thou buildedst not,

Joshua 5:6:

For the children of ISRAEL walked forty years in the wilderness, till all the people that were men of war, which came out of Egypt, were consumed, because they obeyed not the voice of the Lord: unto whom the Lord sware that he would not shew them the land, which the Lord sware unto their fathers that he would give us, a land that floweth with milk and honey.

Judges 2:1:

And an angel of the Lord came up from Gilgal to Bochim, and said, I made you to go up out of Egypt, and have brought you unto the land which I sware unto your fathers; and I said, I will never break my covenant with you.

ISRAEL: The Restoration of the Land

Isaiah 35:1:

The wilderness and the solitary place shall be glad for them; and the desert shall rejoice, and blossom as the rose.

Isaiah 41:19:

I will plant in the wilderness the cedar, the shittah tree, and the myrtle, and the oil tree; I will set in the desert the fir tree, and the pine, and the box tree together:

Isaiah 44:26:

That confirmeth the word of his servant, and performeth the counsel of his messengers; that saith to Jerusalem, Thou shalt be inhabited; and to the cities of Judah, Ye shall be built, and I will raise up the decayed places thereof:

Isaiah 49:19:

For thy waste and thy desolate places, and the land of thy

destruction, shall even now be too narrow by reason of the inhabitants, and they that swallowed thee up shall be far away.

Isaiah 52:9:

Break forth into joy, sing together, ye waste places of Jerusalem: for the Lord hath comforted his people, he hath redeemed Jerusalem.

Isaiah 58:12:

And they that shall be of thee shall build the old waste places: thou shalt raise up the foundations of many generations; and thou shalt be called, The repairer of the breach, The restorer of paths to dwell in.

Isaiah 61:4:

And they shall build the old wastes, they shall raise up the former desolations, and they shall repair the waste cities, the desolations of many generations.

Ezekiel 36:10:

And I will multiply men upon you, all the house of IS-RAEL, even all of it: and the cities shall be inhabited, and the wastes shall be builded:

ISRAEL:
The People and Their Promises

ISRAEL: A Name Given to Jacob

Genesis 32:27-28:

And he said unto him, What is thy name? And he said, Jacob.

And he said, Thy name shall be called no more Jacob, but ISRAEL: for as a prince hast thou power with God and with men, and hast prevailed.

Genesis 35:10:

And God said unto him, Thy name is Jacob: thy name shall not be called any more Jacob, but ISRAEL shall be thy name: and he called his name ISRAEL.

2 Kings 17:34:

Unto this day they do after the former manners: they fear not the Lord, neither do they after their statutes, or after their ordinances, or after the law and commandment which the Lord commanded the children of Jacob, whom he named IS-RAEL;

Isaiah 9:8:

The Lord sent a word into Jacob, and it hath lighted upon ISRAEL.

ISRAEL: A Name Given to the Descendants of Jacob

2 Samuel 7:23:

And what one nation in the earth is like thy people, even like ISRAEL, whom God went to redeem for a people to himself, and to make him a name, and to do for you great things and terrible, for thy land, before thy people, which thou redeemedst to thee from Egypt, from the nations and their gods?

Psalms 135:4:

For the Lord hath chosen Jacob unto himself, and ISRAEL for his peculiar treasure.

Isaiah 43:1:

But now thus saith the Lord that created thee, O Jacob, and he that formed thee, O ISRAEL, Fear not: for I have redeemed thee, I have called thee by thy name; thou art mine.

Isaiah 45:4:

For Jacob my servant's sake, and ISRAEL mine elect, I have even called thee by thy name: I have surnamed thee, though thou hast not known me.

Philippians 3:5:

Circumcised the eighth day, of the stock of ISRAEL, of the tribe of Benjamin, an Hebrew of the Hebrews; as touching the law, a Pharisee;

ISRAEL: A Name Given to Messiah in Prophecy

Isaiah 49:3:

And said unto me, Thou art my servant, O ISRAEL, in whom I will be glorified.

ISRAEL: Other Names of the People

The Ancient People

Isaiah 44:7:

And who, as I, shall call, and shall declare it, and set it in order for me, since I appointed the ancient people? and the things that are coming, and shall come, let them shew unto them.

The Children of ISRAEL

Exodus 1:13:

And the Egyptians made the children of ISRAEL to serve with rigour:

Joshua 13:6:

All the inhabitants of the hill country from Lebanon unto Misrephothmaim, and all the Sidonians, them will I drive out from before the children of ISRAEL: only divide thou it by lot unto the Israelites for an inheritance, as I have commanded thee.

The Elect, His Elect, God's Elect

Matthew 24:22:
And except those days should be shortened, there should no flesh be saved: but for **the elect's** sake those days shall be shortened.

Matthew 24:31:
And he shall send his angels with a great sound of a trumpet, and they shall gather together **his elect** from the four winds, from one end of heaven to the other.

Luke 18:7:
And shall not God avenge **his own elect**, which cry day and night unto him, though he bear long with them?

Romans 8:33:
Who shall lay any thing to the charge of **God's elect?** It is God that justifieth.

2 Timothy 2:10:
Therefore I endure all things for **the elect's** sakes, that they may also obtain the salvation which is in Christ Jesus with eternal glory.

The Hebrews

Exodus 10:3:
And Moses and Aaron came in unto Pharaoh, and said

unto him, Thus saith the Lord God of the Hebrews, How long wilt thou refuse to humble thyself before me? let my people go, that they may serve me.

1 Samuel 4:6:

And when the Philistines heard the noise of the shout, they said, What meaneth the noise of this great shout in the camp of **the Hebrews**? And they understood that the ark of the Lord was come into the camp.

1 Samuel 13:3:

And Jonathan smote the garrison of the Philistines that was in Geba, and the Philistines heard of it. And Saul blew the trumpet throughout all the land, saying, Let **the Hebrews** hear.

The House of Israel

Exodus 40:38:

For the cloud of the Lord was upon the tabernacle by day, and fire was on it by night, in the sight of all **the house of ISRAEL**, throughout all their journeys.

Joshua 21:45:

There failed not ought of any good thing which the Lord had spoken unto **the house of ISRAEL**; all came to pass.

2 Samuel 6:5:

And David and all **the house of ISRAEL** played before the Lord on all manner of instruments made of fir wood, even on harps, and on psalteries, and on timbrels, and on cornets, and on cymbals.

2 Samuel 6:15:
So David and all **the house of ISRAEL** brought up the ark of the Lord with shouting, and with the sound of the trumpet.

Psalms 98:3:
He hath remembered his mercy and his truth toward **the house of ISRAEL**: all the ends of the earth have seen the salvation of our God.

Psalms 115:12:
The Lord hath been mindful of us: he will bless us; he will bless **the house of ISRAEL**; he will bless the house of Aaron.

Psalms 135:19:
Bless the Lord, O **house of ISRAEL**: bless the Lord, O house of Aaron:

Isaiah 5:7:
For the vineyard of the Lord of hosts is **the house of ISRAEL**, and the men of Judah his pleasant plant: and he looked for judgment, but behold oppression; for righteousness, but behold a cry.

Isaiah 63:7:
I will mention the lovingkindnesses of the Lord, and the

praises of the Lord, according to all that the Lord hath bestowed on us, and the great goodness toward **the house of ISRAEL**, which he hath bestowed on them according to his mercies, and according to the multitude of his lovingkindnesses.

Jeremiah 18:6:

O **house of ISRAEL**, cannot I do with you as this potter? saith the Lord. Behold, as the clay is in the potter's hand, so are ye in mine hand, O **house of ISRAEL.**

Jeremiah 31:31:

Behold, the days come, saith the Lord, that I will make a new covenant with **the house of ISRAEL**, and with the house of Judah:

Jeremiah 31:33:

But this shall be the covenant that I will make with **the house of ISRAEL**; After those days, saith the Lord, I will put my law in their inward parts, and write it in their hearts; and will be their God, and they shall be my people.

Jeremiah 33:14:

Behold, the days come, saith the Lord, that I will perform that good thing which I have promised unto **the house of ISRAEL** and to the house of Judah.

Amos 5:4:

For thus saith the Lord unto **the house of ISRAEL**, Seek ye me, and ye shall live:

Hebrews 8:8:

For finding fault with them, he saith, Behold, the days come, saith the Lord, when I will make a new covenant with **the house of ISRAEL** and with the house of Judah:

An Holy People

Deuteronomy 7:6:

For thou art **an holy people** unto the Lord thy God: the Lord thy God hath chosen thee to be a special people unto himself, above all people that are upon the face of the earth.

Deuteronomy 14:2:

For thou art **an holy people** unto the Lord thy God, and the Lord hath chosen thee to be a peculiar people unto himself, above all the nations that are upon the earth.

Deuteronomy 14:21:

Ye shall not eat of any thing that dieth of itself: thou shalt give it unto the stranger that is in thy gates, that he may eat it; or thou mayest sell it unto an alien: for thou art **an holy people** unto the Lord thy God.

The ISRAELites

Exodus 9:7:

And Pharaoh sent, and, behold, there was not one of the cattle of **the ISRAELites** dead. And the heart of Pharaoh was hardened, and he did not let the people go.

Leviticus 23:42:

Ye shall dwell in booths seven days; all that are **ISRAEL-ites** born shall dwell in booths:

Numbers 25:14:

Now the name of **the ISRAELite** that was slain, even that was slain with the Midianitish woman, was Zimri, the son of Salu, a prince of a chief house among the Simeonites.

2 Samuel 17:25:

And Absalom made Amasa captain of the host instead of Joab: which Amasa was a man's son, whose name was Ithra **an ISRAELite**, that went in to Abigail the daughter of Nahash, sister to Zeruiah Joab's mother.

John 1:47:

Jesus saw Nathanael coming to him, and saith of him, Behold **an ISRAELite** indeed, in whom is no guile!

Romans 9:4:

Who are **ISRAELites**; to whom pertaineth the adoption, and the glory, and the covenants, and the giving of the law, and the service of God, and the promises;

Romans 11:1:

I say then, Hath God cast away his people? God forbid. For I also am **an ISRAELite**, of the seed of Abraham, of the tribe of Benjamin.

My People

Exodus 3:7:

And the Lord said, I have surely seen the affliction of **my people** which are in Egypt, and have heard their cry by reason of their taskmasters; for I know their sorrows;

Exodus 10:3:

And Moses and Aaron came in unto Pharaoh, and said unto him, Thus saith the Lord God of the Hebrews, How long wilt thou refuse to humble thyself before me? let **my people** go, that they may serve me.

My Son, My Firstborn

Exodus 4:22-23:

And thou shalt say unto Pharaoh, Thus saith the Lord, ISRAEL is **my son**, even **my firstborn**:

And I say unto thee, Let **my son** go, that he may serve me: and if thou refuse to let him go, behold, I will slay thy son, even thy firstborn.

A Peculiar Treasure

Exodus 19:5:

Now therefore, if ye will obey my voice indeed, and keep my covenant, then ye shall be **a peculiar treasure** unto me above all people: for all the earth is mine:

His Peculiar People

Deuteronomy 26:18:

And the Lord hath avouched thee this day to be **his peculiar people**, as he hath promised thee, and that thou shouldest keep all his commandments;

A People of Inheritance

Deuteronomy 4:20:

But the Lord hath taken you, and brought you forth out of the iron furnace, even out of Egypt, to be unto him **a people of inheritance**, as ye are this day.

A Special People

Deuteronomy 7:6:

For thou art an holy people unto the Lord thy God: the Lord thy God hath chosen thee to be **a special people** unto himself, above all people that are upon the face of the earth.

ISRAEL: Prophecies Given to the Patriarchs Concerning the People

Genesis 15:5:

And he brought him forth abroad, and said, Look now toward heaven, and tell the stars, if thou be able to number them: and he said unto him, So shall thy seed be.

Genesis 15:13-14:

And he said unto Abram, Know of a surety that thy seed

shall be a stranger in a land that is not theirs, and shall serve them; and they shall afflict them four hundred years;

And also that nation, whom they shall serve, will I judge: and afterward shall they come out with great substance.

Genesis 26:4:

And I will make thy seed to multiply as the stars of heaven, and will give unto thy seed all these countries; and in thy seed shall all the nations of the earth be blessed;

Genesis 27:28-29:

Therefore God give thee of the dew of heaven, and the fatness of the earth, and plenty of corn and wine:

Let people serve thee, and nations bow down to thee: be lord over thy brethren, and let thy mother's sons bow down to thee: cursed be every one that curseth thee, and blessed be he that blesseth thee.

ISRAEL: A Prophetic Benediction Given to Moses on Behalf of the People

Numbers 6:22-27:

And the Lord spake unto Moses, saying,

Speak unto Aaron and unto his sons, saying, On this wise ye shall bless the children of ISRAEL, saying unto them,

The Lord bless thee, and keep thee:

The Lord make his face shine upon thee, and be gracious unto thee:

The Lord lift up his countenance upon thee, and give thee peace.

And they shall put my name upon the children of ISRAEL, and I will bless them.

ISRAEL: the Uniqueness of the People

ISRAEL: A People Chosen by God

Exodus 6:7:
And I will take you to me for a people, and I will be to you a God: and ye shall know that I am the Lord your God, which bringeth you out from under the burdens of the Egyptians.

Exodus 29:45-46:
And I will dwell among the children of ISRAEL, and will be their God.

And they shall know that I am the Lord their God, that brought them forth out of the land of Egypt, that I may dwell among them: I am the Lord their God.

Deuteronomy 4:37:
And because he loved thy fathers, therefore he chose their seed after them, and brought thee out in his sight with his mighty power out of Egypt;

Deuteronomy 7:6-8:
For thou art an holy people unto the Lord thy God: the Lord thy God hath chosen thee to be a special people unto himself, above all people that are upon the face of the earth.

The Lord did not set his love upon you, nor choose you, because ye were more in number than any people; for ye were the fewest of all people:

But because the Lord loved you, and because he would keep the oath which he had sworn unto your fathers, hath the

Lord brought you out with a mighty hand, and redeemed you out of the house of bondmen, from the hand of Pharaoh king of Egypt.

Deuteronomy 14:2:

For thou art an holy people unto the Lord thy God, and the Lord hath chosen thee to be a peculiar people unto himself, above all the nations that are upon the earth.

1 Samuel 12:22:

For the Lord will not forsake his people for his great name's sake: because it hath pleased the Lord to make you his people.

Isaiah 48:12:

Hearken unto me, O Jacob and Israel, my called; I am he; I am the first, I also am the last.

Isaiah 51:15-16:

But I am the Lord thy God, that divided the sea, whose waves roared: The Lord of hosts is his name.

And I have put my words in thy mouth, and I have covered thee in the shadow of mine hand, that I may plant the heavens, and lay the foundations of the earth, and say unto Zion, Thou art my people.

ISRAEL: A People Exalted Above All Nations

Deuteronomy 26:19:

And to make thee high above all nations which he hath

made, in praise, and in name, and in honour; and that thou mayest be an holy people unto the Lord thy God, as he hath spoken.

ISRAEL: A People Guided Like a Flock

Psalms 78:52:

But made his own people to go forth like sheep, and guided them in the wilderness like a flock.

Psalms 100:3:

Know ye that the Lord he is God: it is he that hath made us, and not we ourselves; we are his people, and the sheep of his pasture.

Jeremiah 33:12-13:

Thus saith the Lord of hosts; Again in this place, which is desolate without man and without beast, and in all the cities thereof, shall be an habitation of shepherds causing their flocks to lie down.

In the cities of the mountains, in the cities of the vale, and in the cities of the south, and in the land of Benjamin, and in the places about Jerusalem, and in the cities of Judah, shall the flocks pass again under the hands of him that telleth them, saith the Lord.

Ezekiel 36:37-38:

Thus saith the Lord God; I will yet for this be inquired of by the house of Israel, to do it for them; I will increase them with men like a flock.

As the holy flock, as the flock of Jerusalem in her solemn feasts; so shall the waste cities be filled with flocks of men: and they shall know that I am the Lord.

Micah 2:12:

I will surely assemble, O Jacob, all of thee; I will surely gather the remnant of ISRAEL; I will put them together as the sheep of Bozrah, as the flock in the midst of their fold: they shall make great noise by reason of the multitude of men.

Micah 4:8:

And thou, O tower of the flock, the strong hold of the daughter of Zion, unto thee shall it come, even the first dominion; the kingdom shall come to the daughter of Jerusalem.

Zechariah 9:16:

And the Lord their God shall save them in that day as the flock of his people: for they shall be as the stones of a crown, lifted up as an ensign upon his land.

ISRAEL: A People Who Have the Law of God Written Upon Their Hearts

Jeremiah 31:31-34:

Behold, the days come, saith the Lord, that I will make a new covenant with the house of Israel, and with the house of Judah:

Not according to the covenant that I made with their fathers in the day that I took them by the hand to bring them out of the land of Egypt; which my covenant they brake, although I was an husband unto them, saith the Lord:

But this shall be the covenant that I will make with the house of Israel; After those days, saith the Lord, I will put my law in their inward parts, and write it in their hearts; and will be their God, and they shall be my people.

And they shall teach no more every man his neighbour, and every man his brother, saying, Know the Lord: for they shall all know me, from the least of them unto the greatest of them, saith the Lord: for I will forgive their iniquity, and I will remember their sin no more.

Hebrews 8:10:

For this is the covenant that I will make with the house of ISRAEL after those days, saith the Lord; I will put my laws into their mind, and write them in their hearts: and I will be to them a God, and they shall be to me a people:

ISRAEL: A People That Is Firmly Established

Deuteronomy 28:9:

The Lord shall establish thee an holy people unto himself, as he hath sworn unto thee, if thou shalt keep the commandments of the Lord thy God, and walk in his ways.

2 Chronicles 9:8:

Blessed be the Lord thy God, which delighted in thee to set thee on his throne, to be king for the Lord thy God: because thy God loved Israel, to establish them for ever, therefore made he thee king over them, to do judgment and justice.

2 Chronicles 20:20:

And they rose early in the morning, and went forth into

the wilderness of Tekoa: and as they went forth, Jehoshaphat stood and said, Hear me, O Judah, and ye inhabitants of Jerusalem; Believe in the Lord your God, so shall ye be established; believe his prophets, so shall ye prosper.

Isaiah 54:14:

In righteousness shalt thou be established: thou shalt be far from oppression; for thou shalt not fear: and from terror; for it shall not come near thee.

ISRAEL: A People That Cannot Be moved

Psalms 46:5:

God is in the midst of her; she shall not be moved: God shall help her, and that right early.

Psalms 121:3-4:

He will not suffer thy foot to be moved: he that keepeth thee will not slumber.

Behold, he that keepeth Israel shall neither slumber nor sleep.

Psalms 125:1:

They that trust in the Lord shall be as mount Zion, which cannot be removed, but abideth for ever.

ISRAEL: A People That Was Blessed, Even in Captivity

Exodus 1:7:

And the children of ISRAEL were fruitful, and increased

abundantly, and multiplied, and waxed exceeding mighty; and the land was filled with them.

Leviticus 26:44-45:

And yet for all that, when they be in the land of their enemies, I will not cast them away, neither will I abhor them, to destroy them utterly, and to break my covenant with them: for I am the Lord their God.

But I will for their sakes remember the covenant of their ancestors, whom I brought forth out of the land of Egypt in the sight of the heathen, that I might be their God: I am the Lord.

ISRAEL: A People That Was Exempt From the Plagues of Egypt and Immune to Calamities

Exodus 8:22-23:

And I will sever in that day the land of Goshen, in which my people dwell, that no swarms of flies shall be there; to the end thou mayest know that I am the Lord in the midst of the earth.

And I will put a division between my people and thy people: to morrow shall this sign be.

Exodus 9:6:

And the Lord did that thing on the morrow, and all the cattle of Egypt died: but of the cattle of the children of IS-RAEL died not one.

Exodus 9:26:

Only in the land of Goshen, where the children of IS-RAEL were, was there no hail.

Exodus 10:21-23:

And the Lord said unto Moses, Stretch out thine hand toward heaven, that there may be darkness over the land of Egypt, even darkness which may be felt.

And Moses stretched forth his hand toward heaven; and there was a thick darkness in all the land of Egypt three days:

They saw not one another, neither rose any from his place for three days: but all the children of ISRAEL had light in their dwellings.

Exodus 11:7:

But against any of the children of ISRAEL shall not a dog move his tongue, against man or beast: that ye may know how that the Lord doth put a difference between the Egyptians and ISRAEL.

Exodus 12:13:

And the blood shall be to you for a token upon the houses where ye are: and when I see the blood, I will pass over you, and the plague shall not be upon you to destroy you, when I smite the land of Egypt.

Exodus 15:26:

I will put none of these diseases upon thee, which I have brought upon the Egyptians: for I am the Lord that healeth thee.

Psalms 91:7:

A thousand shall fall at thy side, and ten thousand at thy right hand; but it shall not come nigh thee.

ISRAEL: A People That Is Promised Health

Exodus 15:26:

And said, If thou wilt diligently hearken to the voice of the Lord thy God, and wilt do that which is right in his sight, and wilt give ear to his commandments, and keep all his statutes, I will put none of these diseases upon thee, which I have brought upon the Egyptians: for I am the Lord that healeth thee.

Exodus 23:25:

And I will take sickness away from the midst of thee.

Deuteronomy 7:15:

And the Lord will take away from thee all sickness, and will put none of the evil diseases of Egypt, which thou knowest, upon thee; but will lay them upon all them that hate thee.

Proverbs 4:20-22:

My son, attend to my words; incline thine ear unto my sayings.

Let them not depart from thine eyes; keep them in the midst of thine heart.

For they are life unto those that find them, and health to all their flesh.

Jeremiah 30:17:

For I will restore health unto thee, and I will heal thee of thy wounds, saith the Lord;

ISRAEL: A People That Is Promised Protection

Exodus 23:20:
Behold, I send an Angel before thee, to keep thee in the way, and to bring thee into the place which I have prepared.

Psalms 125:2:
As the mountains are round about Jerusalem, so the Lord is round about his people from henceforth even for ever.

Zechariah 2:5:
For I, saith the Lord, will be unto her a wall of fire round about, and will be the glory in the midst of her.

ISRAEL: A People That Is Promised Prosperity

Deuteronomy 28:2:
And all these blessings shall come on thee, and overtake thee, if thou shalt hearken unto the voice of the Lord thy God.

Deuteronomy 28:8:
The Lord shall command the blessing upon thee in thy storehouses, and in all that thou settest thine hand unto; and he shall bless thee in the land which the Lord thy God giveth thee.

Deuteronomy 28:11-12:
And the Lord shall make thee plenteous in goods, in the fruit of thy body, and in the fruit of thy cattle, and in the fruit

of thy ground, in the land which the Lord sware unto thy fathers to give thee.

The Lord shall open unto thee his good treasure, the heaven to give the rain unto thy land in his season, and to bless all the work of thine hand: and thou shalt lend unto many nations, and thou shalt not borrow.

Deuteronomy 30:9:

And the Lord thy God will make thee plenteous in every work of thine hand, in the fruit of thy body, and in the fruit of thy cattle, and in the fruit of thy land, for good: for the Lord will again rejoice over thee for good, as he rejoiced over thy fathers:

Zechariah 8:12-13:

For the seed shall be prosperous; the vine shall give her fruit, and the ground shall give her increase, and the heavens shall give their dew; and I will cause the remnant of this people to possess all these things.

And it shall come to pass, that as ye were a curse among the heathen, O house of Judah, and house of Israel; so will I save you, and ye shall be a blessing: fear not, but let your hands be strong.

ISRAEL: A People That Is Promised Exaltation and Greatness

Ezekiel 37:26:

Moreover I will make a covenant of peace with them; it shall be an everlasting covenant with them: and I will place them, and multiply them, and will set my sanctuary in the midst of them for evermore.

Isaiah 2:2-4:

And it shall come to pass in the last days, that the mountain of the Lord's house shall be established in the top of the mountains, and shall be exalted above the hills; and all nations shall flow unto it.

And many people shall go and say, Come ye, and let us go up to the mountain of the Lord, to the house of the God of Jacob; and he will teach us of his ways, and we will walk in his paths: for out of Zion shall go forth the law, and the word of the Lord from Jerusalem.

And he shall judge among the nations, and shall rebuke many people: and they shall beat their swords into plowshares, and their spears into pruninghooks: nation shall not lift up sword against nation, neither shall they learn war any more.

Isaiah 9:6-7:

For unto us a child is born, unto us a son is given: and the government shall be upon his shoulder: and his name shall be called Wonderful, Counsellor, The mighty God, the everlasting Father, The Prince of Peace.

Of the increase of his government and peace there shall be no end, upon the throne of David, and upon his kingdom, to order it, and to establish it with judgment and with justice from henceforth even for ever. The zeal of the Lord of hosts will perform this.

Hosea 2:19-20:

And I will betroth thee unto me for ever; yea, I will betroth thee unto me in righteousness, and in judgment, and in lovingkindness, and in mercies.

I will even betroth thee unto me in faithfulness: and thou shalt know the Lord.

Zephaniah 3:14-20:

Sing, O daughter of Zion; shout, O ISRAEL; be glad and rejoice with all the heart, O daughter of Jerusalem.

The Lord hath taken away thy judgments, he hath cast out thine enemy: the king of ISRAEL, even the Lord, is in the midst of thee: thou shalt not see evil any more.

In that day it shall be said to Jerusalem, Fear thou not: and to Zion, Let not thine hands be slack.

The Lord thy God in the midst of thee is mighty; he will save, he will rejoice over thee with joy; he will rest in his love, he will joy over thee with singing.

I will gather them that are sorrowful for the solemn assembly, who are of thee, to whom the reproach of it was a burden.

Behold, at that time I will undo all that afflict thee: and I will save her that halteth, and gather her that was driven out; and I will get them praise and fame in every land where they have been put to shame.

At that time will I bring you again, even in the time that I gather you: for I will make you a name and a praise among all people of the earth, when I turn back your captivity before your eyes, saith the Lord.

Zechariah 8:23:

Thus saith the Lord of hosts; In those days it shall come to pass, that ten men shall take hold out of all languages of the nations, even shall take hold of the skirt of him that is a Jew, saying, We will go with you: for we have heard that God is with you.

Zechariah 14:16:

And it shall come to pass, that every one that is left of all the nations which came against Jerusalem shall even go up from year to year to worship the King, the Lord of hosts, and to keep the feast of tabernacles.

ISRAEL: A People That Is Promised Strength and Peace

Leviticus 26:6:

And I will give **peace** in the land, and ye shall lie down, and none shall make you afraid: and I will rid evil beasts out of the land, neither shall the sword go through your land.

Psalms 29:11:

The Lord will give **strength** unto his people; the Lord will bless his people with **peace.**

Psalms 72:7:

In his days shall the righteous flourish; and abundance of **peace** so long as the moon endureth.

Psalms 84:5:

Blessed is the man whose **strength** is in thee; in whose heart are the ways of them.

Psalms 84:7:

They go from **strength** to **strength**, every one of them in Zion appeareth before God.

Psalms 85:8:

I will hear what God the Lord will speak: for he will speak **peace** unto his people, and to his saints:

Psalms 128:6:

Yea, thou shalt see thy children's children, and **peace** upon Israel.

Isaiah 26:12:

Lord, thou wilt ordain **peace** for us: for thou also hast wrought all our works in us.

ISRAEL: A Remnant of the People Will Be Saved

Isaiah 1:9:

Except the Lord of hosts had left unto us **a very small remnant**, we should have been as Sodom, and we should have been like unto Gomorrah.

Isaiah 11:11:

And it shall come to pass in that day, that the Lord shall set his hand again the second time to recover **the remnant** of his people, which shall be left, from Assyria, and from Egypt, and from Pathros, and from Cush, and from Elam, and from Shinar, and from Hamath, and from the islands of the sea.

Isaiah 11:16:

And there shall be an highway for **the remnant** of his people, which shall be left, from Assyria; like as it was to ISRAEL in the day that he came up out of the land of Egypt.

Isaiah 37:4:

It may be the Lord thy God will hear the words of Rabshakeh, whom the king of Assyria his master hath sent to reproach the living God, and will reprove the words which the Lord thy God hath heard: wherefore lift up thy prayer for **the remnant** that is left.

Isaiah 37:31-32:

And the **remnant** that is escaped of the house of Judah shall again take root downward, and bear fruit upward:

For out of Jerusalem shall go forth a **remnant**, and they that escape out of mount Zion: the zeal of the Lord of hosts shall do this.

Jeremiah 6:9:

Thus saith the Lord of hosts, They shall throughly glean **the remnant** of ISRAEL as a vine: turn back thine hand as a grapegatherer into the baskets.

Jeremiah 23:3:

And I will gather **the remnant** of my flock out of all countries whither I have driven them, and will bring them again to their folds; and they shall be fruitful and increase.

Jeremiah 31:7:

For thus saith the Lord; Sing with gladness for Jacob, and

shout among the chief of the nations: publish ye, praise ye, and say, O Lord, save thy people, **the remnant** of ISRAEL.

Jeremiah 44:28:

Yet a small number that escape the sword shall return out of the land of Egypt into the land of Judah, and all **the remnant** of Judah, that are gone into the land of Egypt to sojourn there, shall know whose words shall stand, mine, or theirs.

Ezekiel 14:22:

Yet, behold, therein shall be left **a remnant** that shall be brought forth, both sons and daughters: behold, they shall come forth unto you:

Micah 2:12:

I will surely assemble, O Jacob, all of thee; I will surely gather **the remnant** of ISRAEL; I will put them together as the sheep of Bozrah, as the flock in the midst of their fold: they shall make great noise by reason of the multitude of men.

Micah 5:3:

Therefore will he give them up, until the time that she which travaileth hath brought forth: then the remnant of his brethren shall return unto the children of Israel.

Zephaniah 2:7:

And the coast shall be for the remnant of the house of Judah; they shall feed thereupon: in the houses of Ashkelon shall they lie down in the evening: for the Lord their God shall visit them, and turn away their captivity.

Zephaniah 2:9:

Therefore as I live, saith the Lord of hosts, the God of ISRAEL, Surely Moab shall be as Sodom, and the children of Ammon as Gomorrah, even the breeding of nettles, and saltpits, and a perpetual desolation: the residue of my people shall spoil them, and **the remnant** of my people shall possess them.

Romans 9:27:

Esaias also crieth concerning ISRAEL, Though the number of the children of ISRAEL be as the sand of the sea, **a remnant** shall be saved:

Romans 11:5:

Even so then at this present time also there is **a remnant** according to the election of grace.

ISRAEL and STRANGERS

Acceptance of STRANGERS

Exodus 22:21:

Thou shalt neither vex a STRANGER, nor oppress him: for ye were STRANGERS in the land of Egypt.

Exodus 23:9:

Also thou shalt not oppress a STRANGER: for ye know the heart of a STRANGER, seeing ye were STRANGERS in the land of Egypt.

Leviticus 19:33-34:

And if a STRANGER sojourn with thee in your land, ye shall not vex him.

But the STRANGER that dwelleth with you shall be unto you as one born among you, and thou shalt love him as thyself; for ye were STRANGERS in the land of Egypt: I am the Lord your God.

Numbers 15:15:

One ordinance shall be both for you of the congregation, and also for the STRANGER that sojourneth with you, an ordinance for ever in your generations: as ye are, so shall the STRANGER be before the Lord.

Deuteronomy 10:19:

Love ye therefore the STRANGER: for ye were STRANGERS in the land of Egypt.

Deuteronomy 23:7:

Thou shalt not abhor an Edomite; for he is thy brother: thou shalt not abhor an Egyptian; because thou wast a STRANGER in his land.

Ruth 2:10:

Then she fell on her face, and bowed herself to the ground, and said unto him, Why have I found grace in thine eyes, that thou shouldest take knowledge of me, seeing I am a STRANGER?

2 Chronicles 2:17:

And Solomon numbered all the STRANGERS that were in the land of Israel, after the numbering wherewith David his father had numbered them; and they were found an hundred and fifty thousand and three thousand and six hundred.

2 Chronicles 15:9:

And he gathered all Judah and Benjamin, and the STRANGERS with them out of Ephraim and Manasseh, and out of

Simeon: for they fell to him out of Israel in abundance, when they saw that the Lord his God was with him.

Isaiah 14:1:

For the Lord will have mercy on Jacob, and will yet choose Israel, and set them in their own land: and the STRANGERS shall be joined with them, and they shall cleave to the house of Jacob.

Hebrews 13:2:

Be not forgetful to entertain STRANGERS: for thereby some have entertained angels unawares.

Justice for STRANGERS

Numbers 15:16:

One law and one manner shall be for you, and for the STRANGER that sojourneth with you.

Numbers 15:26:

And it shall be forgiven all the congregation of the children of Israel, and the STRANGER that sojourneth among them; seeing all the people were in ignorance.

Numbers 35:15:

These six cities shall be a refuge, both for the children of Israel, and for the STRANGER, and for the sojourner among them: that every one that killeth any person unawares may flee thither.

Deuteronomy 1:16:
And I charged your judges at that time, saying, Hear the causes between your brethren, and judge righteously between every man and his brother, and the STRANGER that is with him.

Deuteronomy 24:17:
Thou shalt not pervert the judgment of the STRANGER, nor of the fatherless; nor take a widow's raiment to pledge:

Deuteronomy 27:19:
Cursed be he that perverteth the judgment of the STRANGER, fatherless, and widow. And all the people shall say, Amen.

Joshua 20:9:
These were the cities appointed for all the children of Israel, and for the STRANGER that sojourneth among them, that whosoever killeth any person at unawares might flee thither, and not die by the hand of the avenger of blood, until he stood before the congregation.

Jeremiah 7:6-7:
If ye oppress not the STRANGER, the fatherless, and the widow, and shed not innocent blood in this place, neither walk after other gods to your hurt:
Then will I cause you to dwell in this place, in the land that I gave to your fathers, for ever and ever.

Jeremiah 22:3:
Thus saith the Lord; Execute ye judgment and righteous-

ness, and deliver the spoiled out of the hand of the oppressor: and do no wrong, do no violence to the STRANGER, the fatherless, nor the widow, neither shed innocent blood in this place.

Ezekiel 22:29:

The people of the land have used oppression, and exercised robbery, and have vexed the poor and needy: yea, they have oppressed the STRANGER wrongfully.

Zechariah 7:10:

And oppress not the widow, nor the fatherless, the STRANGER, nor the poor; and let none of you imagine evil against his brother in your heart.

Malachi 3:5:

And I will come near to you to judgment; and I will be a swift witness against the sorcerers, and against the adulterers, and against false swearers, and against those that oppress the hireling in his wages, the widow, and the fatherless, and that turn aside the STRANGER from his right, and fear not me, saith the Lord of hosts.

Provision for STRANGERS

Leviticus 19:10:

And thou shalt not glean thy vineyard, neither shalt thou gather every grape of thy vineyard; thou shalt leave them for the poor and STRANGER: I am the Lord your God.

Leviticus 23:22:
And when ye reap the harvest of your land, thou shalt not make clean riddance of the corners of thy field when thou reapest, neither shalt thou gather any gleaning of thy harvest: thou shalt leave them unto the poor, and to the STRANGER: I am the Lord your God.

Leviticus 25:35:
And if thy brother be waxen poor, and fallen in decay with thee; then thou shalt relieve him: yea, though he be a STRANGER, or a sojourner; that he may live with thee.

Deuteronomy 10:18:
He doth execute the judgment of the fatherless and widow, and loveth the STRANGER, in giving him food and raiment.

Deuteronomy 24:14:
Thou shalt not oppress an hired servant that is poor and needy, whether he be of thy brethren, or of thy STRANGERS that are in thy land within thy gates:

Deuteronomy 24:19-21:
When thou cuttest down thine harvest in thy field, and hast forgot a sheaf in the field, thou shalt not go again to fetch it: it shall be for the STRANGER, for the fatherless, and for the widow: that the Lord thy God may bless thee in all the work of thine hands.

When thou beatest thine olive tree, thou shalt not go over the boughs again: it shall be for the STRANGER, for the fatherless, and for the widow.

When thou gatherest the grapes of thy vineyard, thou

shalt not glean it afterward: it shall be for the STRANGER, for the fatherless, and for the widow.

Deuteronomy 26:12-13:
When thou hast made an end of tithing all the tithes of thine increase the third year, which is the year of tithing, and hast given it unto the Levite, the STRANGER, the fatherless, and the widow, that they may eat within thy gates, and be filled;

Then thou shalt say before the Lord thy God, I have brought away the hallowed things out of mine house, and also have given them unto the Levite, and unto the STRANGER, to the fatherless, and to the widow, according to all thy commandments which thou hast commanded me: I have not transgressed thy commandments, neither have I forgotten them.

Job 31:32:
The STRANGER did not lodge in the street: but I opened my doors to the traveller.

Psalms146:9:
The Lord preserveth the STRANGERS; he relieveth the fatherless and widow: but the way of the wicked he turneth upside down.

Ezekiel 47:22-23:
And it shall come to pass, that ye shall divide it by lot for an inheritance unto you, and to the STRANGERS that so-

journ among you, which shall beget children among you: and they shall be unto you as born in the country among the children of Israel; they shall have inheritance with you among the tribes of Israel.

And it shall come to pass, that in what tribe the STRANGER sojourneth, there shall ye give him his inheritance, saith the Lord God.

Worshipping With STRANGERS

Deuteronomy 16:11:

And thou shalt rejoice before the Lord thy God, thou, and thy son, and thy daughter, and thy manservant, and thy maidservant, and the Levite that is within thy gates, and the STRANGER, and the fatherless, and the widow, that are among you, in the place which the Lord thy God hath chosen to place his name there.

Deuteronomy 16:14:

And thou shalt rejoice in thy feast, thou, and thy son, and thy daughter, and thy manservant, and thy maidservant, and the Levite, the STRANGER, and the fatherless, and the widow, that are within thy gates.

Deuteronomy 26:11:

And thou shalt rejoice in every good thing which the Lord thy God hath given unto thee, and unto thine house, thou, and the Levite, and the STRANGER that is among you.

Deuteronomy 29:10-13:

Ye stand this day all of you before the Lord your God;

your captains of your tribes, your elders, and your officers, with all the men of Israel,

Your little ones, your wives, and thy STRANGER that is in thy camp, from the hewer of thy wood unto the drawer of thy water:

That thou shouldest enter into covenant with the Lord thy God, and into his oath, which the Lord thy God maketh with thee this day:

That he may establish thee to day for a people unto himself, and that he may be unto thee a God, as he hath said unto thee, and as he hath sworn unto thy fathers, to Abraham, to Isaac, and to Jacob.

Deuteronomy 31:12:

Gather the people together, men and women, and children, and thy STRANGER that is within thy gates, that they may hear, and that they may learn, and fear the Lord your God, and observe to do all the words of this law:

Joshua 8:33:

And all Israel, and their elders, and officers, and their judges, stood on this side the ark and on that side before the priests the Levites, which bare the ark of the covenant of the Lord, as well the STRANGER, as he that was born among them; half of them over against mount Gerizim, and half of them over against mount Ebal; as Moses the servant of the Lord had commanded before, that they should bless the people of Israel.

Joshua 8:35:

There was not a word of all that Moses commanded, which

Joshua read not before all the congregation of Israel, with the women, and the little ones, and the STRANGERS that were conversant among them.

1 Kings 8:41-43:

Moreover concerning a STRANGER, that is not of thy people Israel, but cometh out of a far country for thy name's sake;

(For they shall hear of thy great name, and of thy strong hand, and of thy stretched out arm;) when he shall come and pray toward this house;

Hear thou in heaven thy dwelling place, and do according to all that the STRANGER calleth to thee for: that all people of the earth may know thy name, to fear thee, as do thy people Israel; and that they may know that this house, which I have builded, is called by thy name.

2 Chronicles 6:32-33:

Moreover concerning the STRANGER, which is not of thy people Israel, but is come from a far country for thy great name's sake, and thy mighty hand, and thy stretched out arm; if they come and pray in this house;

Then hear thou from the heavens, even from thy dwelling place, and do according to all that the STRANGER calleth to thee for; that all people of the earth may know thy name, and fear thee, as doth thy people Israel, and may know that this house which I have built is called by thy name.

2 Chronicles 30:25:

And all the congregation of Judah, with the priests and the Levites, and all the congregation that came out of Israel, and the STRANGERS that came out of the land of Israel, and that dwelt in Judah, rejoiced.

Strangers and Restoration

Isaiah 60:10:

And the sons of STRANGERS shall build up thy walls, and their kings shall minister unto thee: for in my wrath I smote thee, but in my favour have I had mercy on thee.

Isaiah 61:5:

And STRANGERS shall stand and feed your flocks, and the sons of the alien shall be your plowmen and your vinedressers.

ISRAEL:
The Nation and Its Promises

ISRAEL: The Salvation and Cleansing of the Nation

Psalms 14:7:

Oh that the salvation of ISRAEL were come out of Zion! when the Lord bringeth back the captivity of his people, Jacob shall rejoice, and ISRAEL shall be glad.

Psalms 51:1-3:

Have mercy upon me, O God, according to thy loving-kindness: according unto the multitude of thy tender mercies blot out my transgressions.

Wash me throughly from mine iniquity, and cleanse me from my sin.

For I acknowledge my transgressions: and my sin is ever before me.

Psalms 53:6:

Oh that the salvation of ISRAEL were come out of Zion!

When God bringeth back the captivity of his people, Jacob shall rejoice, and ISRAEL shall be glad.

Psalms 85:1-9:

Lord, thou hast been favourable unto thy land: thou hast brought back the captivity of Jacob.

Thou hast forgiven the iniquity of thy people, thou hast covered all their sin. Selah.

Thou hast taken away all thy wrath: thou hast turned thyself from the fierceness of thine anger.

Turn us, O God of our salvation, and cause thine anger toward us to cease.

Wilt thou be angry with us for ever? wilt thou draw out thine anger to all generations?

Wilt thou not revive us again: that thy people may rejoice in thee?

Shew us thy mercy, O Lord, and grant us thy salvation.

I will hear what God the Lord will speak: for he will speak peace unto his people, and to his saints: but let them not turn again to folly.

Surely his salvation is nigh them that fear him; that glory may dwell in our land.

Isaiah 44:21-23:

Remember these, O Jacob and ISRAEL; for thou art my servant: I have formed thee; thou art my servant: O ISRAEL, thou shalt not be forgotten of me.

I have blotted out, as a thick cloud, thy transgressions, and, as a cloud, thy sins: return unto me; for I have redeemed thee.

Sing, O ye heavens; for the Lord hath done it: shout, ye lower parts of the earth: break forth into singing, ye mountains, O forest, and every tree therein: for the Lord hath redeemed Jacob, and glorified himself in ISRAEL.

Isaiah 45:17:

But ISRAEL shall be saved in the Lord with an everlasting salvation: ye shall not be ashamed nor confounded world without end.

Isaiah 51:5-6:

My righteousness is near; my salvation is gone forth, and mine arms shall judge the people; the isles shall wait upon me, and on mine arm shall they trust.

Lift up your eyes to the heavens, and look upon the earth beneath: for the heavens shall vanish away like smoke, and the earth shall wax old like a garment, and they that dwell therein shall die in like manner: but my salvation shall be for ever, and my righteousness shall not be abolished.

Isaiah 51:8:

For the moth shall eat them up like a garment, and the worm shall eat them like wool: but my righteousness shall be for ever, and my salvation from generation to generation.

Jeremiah 17:13-14:

O Lord, the hope of ISRAEL, all that forsake thee shall be ashamed, and they that depart from me shall be written in the earth, because they have forsaken the Lord, the fountain of living waters.

Heal me, O Lord, and I shall be healed; save me, and I shall be saved: for thou art my praise.

Jeremiah 50:19-20:

And I will bring ISRAEL again to his habitation, and he shall feed on Carmel and Bashan, and his soul shall be satisfied upon mount Ephraim and Gilead.

In those days, and in that time, saith the Lord, the iniquity of ISRAEL shall be sought for, and there shall be none; and the sins of Judah, and they shall not be found: for I will pardon them whom I reserve.

Daniel 12:1:

And at that time shall Michael stand up, the great prince which standeth for the children of thy people: and there shall be a time of trouble, such as never was since there was a nation even to that same time: and at that time thy people shall be delivered, every one that shall be found written in the book.

Zechariah 12:10:

And I will pour upon the house of David, and upon the inhabitants of Jerusalem, the spirit of grace and of supplications: and they shall look upon me whom they have pierced, and they shall mourn for him, as one mourneth for his only son, and shall be in bitterness for him, as one that is in bitterness for his firstborn.

Zechariah 13:1:

In that day there shall be a fountain opened to the house of

David and to the inhabitants of Jerusalem for sin and for uncleanness.

Romans 11:26-27:

And so all ISRAEL shall be saved: as it is written, There shall come out of Sion the Deliverer, and shall turn away ungodliness from Jacob:

For this is my covenant unto them, when I shall take away their sins.

ISRAEL: The Inheritance of the Nation

Leviticus 20:24:

But I have said unto you, Ye shall inherit their land, and I will give it unto you to possess it, a land that floweth with milk and honey: I am the Lord your God, which have separated you from other people.

Deuteronomy 1:38:

But Joshua the son of Nun, which standeth before thee, he shall go in thither: encourage him: for he shall cause ISRAEL to inherit it.

Joshua 1:6:

Be strong and of a good courage: for unto this people shalt thou divide for an inheritance the land, which I sware unto their fathers to give them.

Joshua 14:2:

By lot was their inheritance, as the Lord commanded by the hand of Moses, for the nine tribes, and for the half tribe.

Isaiah 54:3:

For thou shalt break forth on the right hand and on the left; and thy seed shall inherit the Gentiles [the nations], and make the desolate cities to be inhabited.

Jeremiah 3:19:

But I said, How shall I put thee among the children, and give thee a pleasant land, a goodly heritage of the hosts of nations? and I said, Thou shalt call me, My father; and shalt not turn away from me.

ISRAEL: The Exaltation of the Nation

Deuteronomy 28:1:

And it shall come to pass, if thou shalt hearken diligently unto the voice of the Lord thy God, to observe and to do all his commandments which I command thee this day, that the Lord thy God will set thee on high above all nations of the earth:

Deuteronomy 28:13:

And the Lord shall make thee the head, and not the tail; and thou shalt be above only, and thou shalt not be beneath; if that thou hearken unto the commandments of the Lord thy God, which I command thee this day, to observe and to do them:

Deuteronomy 32:13:

He made him ride on the high places of the earth, that he

might eat the increase of the fields; and he made him to suck honey out of the rock, and oil out of the flinty rock;

Deuteronomy 33:28-29:

ISRAEL then shall dwell in safety alone: the fountain of Jacob shall be upon a land of corn and wine; also his heavens shall drop down dew.

Happy art thou, O ISRAEL: who is like unto thee, O people saved by the Lord, the shield of thy help, and who is the sword of thy excellency! and thine enemies shall be found liars unto thee; and thou shalt tread upon their high places.

Psalms 148:14:

He also exalteth the horn of his people, the praise of all his saints; even of the children of ISRAEL, a people near unto him. Praise ye the Lord.

Isaiah 45:14:

Thus saith the Lord, The labour of Egypt, and merchandise of Ethiopia and of the Sabeans, men of stature, shall come over unto thee, and they shall be thine: they shall come after thee; in chains they shall come over, and they shall fall down unto thee, they shall make supplication unto thee, saying, Surely God is in thee; and there is none else, there is no God.

Isaiah 49:23:

And kings shall be thy nursing fathers, and their queens thy nursing mothers: they shall bow down to thee with their face toward the earth, and lick up the dust of thy feet; and thou

thou shalt know that I am the Lord: for they shall not be ashamed that wait for me.

Micah 4:8:
And thou, O tower of the flock, the strong hold of the daughter of Zion, unto thee shall it come, even the first dominion; the kingdom shall come to the daughter of Jerusalem.

ISRAEL: The Restoration of the Nation

Isaiah 1:25-27:
And I will turn my hand upon thee, and purely purge away thy dross, and take away all thy tin:

And I will restore thy judges as at the first, and thy counsellors as at the beginning: afterward thou shalt be called, The city of righteousness, the faithful city.

Zion shall be redeemed with judgment, and her converts with righteousness.

Isaiah 4:2-6:
In that day shall the branch of the Lord be beautiful and glorious, and the fruit of the earth shall be excellent and comely for them that are escaped of ISRAEL.

And it shall come to pass, that he that is left in Zion, and he that remaineth in Jerusalem, shall be called holy, even every one that is written among the living in Jerusalem:

When the Lord shall have washed away the filth of the daughters of Zion, and shall have purged the blood of Jerusalem from the midst thereof by the spirit of judgment, and by the spirit of burning.

And the Lord will create upon every dwelling place of mount Zion, and upon her assemblies, a cloud and smoke by day, and the shining of a flaming fire by night: for upon all the glory shall be a defence.

And there shall be a tabernacle for a shadow in the daytime from the heat, and for a place of refuge, and for a covert from storm and from rain.

Isaiah 25:6-10:

And in this mountain shall the Lord of hosts make unto all people a feast of fat things, a feast of wines on the lees, of fat things full of marrow, of wines on the lees well refined.

And he will destroy in this mountain the face of the covering cast over all people, and the vail that is spread over all nations.

He will swallow up death in victory; and the Lord God will wipe away tears from off all faces; and the rebuke of his people shall he take away from off all the earth: for the Lord hath spoken it.

And it shall be said in that day, Lo, this is our God; we have waited for him, and he will save us: this is the Lord; we have waited for him, we will be glad and rejoice in his salvation.

For in this mountain shall the hand of the Lord rest.

Isaiah 26:1-2:

In that day shall this song be sung in the land of Judah; We have a strong city; salvation will God appoint for walls and bulwarks.

Open ye the gates, that the righteous nation which keepeth the truth may enter in.

Isaiah 26:12:

Lord, thou wilt ordain peace for us: for thou also hast wrought all our works in us.

Isaiah 29:18-24:

And in that day shall the deaf hear the words of the book, and the eyes of the blind shall see out of obscurity, and out of darkness.

The meek also shall increase their joy in the Lord, and the poor among men shall rejoice in the Holy One of ISRAEL.

For the terrible one is brought to nought, and the scorner is consumed, and all that watch for iniquity are cut off:

That make a man an offender for a word, and lay a snare for him that reproveth in the gate, and turn aside the just for a thing of nought.

Therefore thus saith the Lord, who redeemed Abraham, concerning the house of Jacob, Jacob shall not now be ashamed, neither shall his face now wax pale.

But when he seeth his children, the work of mine hands, in the midst of him, they shall sanctify my name, and sanctify the Holy One of Jacob, and shall fear the God of ISRAEL.

They also that erred in spirit shall come to understanding, and they that murmured shall learn doctrine.

Isaiah 30:18-21:

And therefore will the Lord wait, that he may be gracious unto you, and therefore will he be exalted, that he may have mercy upon you: for the Lord is a God of judgment: blessed are all they that wait for him.

For the people shall dwell in Zion at Jerusalem: thou shalt weep no more: he will be very gracious unto thee at the voice of thy cry; when he shall hear it, he will answer thee.

And though the Lord give you the bread of adversity, and the water of affliction, yet shall not thy teachers be removed into a corner any more, but thine eyes shall see thy teachers:

And thine ears shall hear a word behind thee, saying, This is the way, walk ye in it, when ye turn to the right hand, and when ye turn to the left.

Isaiah 30:23-26:

Then shall he give the rain of thy seed, that thou shalt sow the ground withal; and bread of the increase of the earth, and it shall be fat and plenteous: in that day shall thy cattle feed in large pastures.

The oxen likewise and the young asses that ear the ground shall eat clean provender, which hath been winnowed with the shovel and with the fan.

And there shall be upon every high mountain, and upon every high hill, rivers and streams of waters in the day of the great slaughter, when the towers fall.

Moreover the light of the moon shall be as the light of the sun, and the light of the sun shall be sevenfold, as the light of seven days, in the day that the Lord bindeth up the breach of his people, and healeth the stroke of their wound.

Isaiah 32:15-18:

Until the spirit be poured upon us from on high, and the

wilderness be a fruitful field, and the fruitful field be counted for a forest.

Then judgment shall dwell in the wilderness, and righteousness remain in the fruitful field.

And the work of righteousness shall be peace; and the effect of righteousness quietness and assurance for ever.

And my people shall dwell in a peaceable habitation, and in sure dwellings, and in quiet resting places;

Isaiah 33:24:

And the inhabitant shall not say, I am sick: the people that dwell therein shall be forgiven their iniquity.

Isaiah 35:1-2:

The wilderness and the solitary place shall be glad for them; and the desert shall rejoice, and blossom as the rose.

It shall blossom abundantly, and rejoice even with joy and singing: the glory of Lebanon shall be given unto it, the excellency of Carmel and Sharon, they shall see the glory of the Lord, and the excellency of our God.

Isaiah 35:3-6:

Strengthen ye the weak hands, and confirm the feeble knees.

Say to them that are of a fearful heart, Be strong, fear not: behold, your God will come with vengeance, even God with a recompence; he will come and save you.

Then the eyes of the blind shall be opened, and the ears of the deaf shall be unstopped.

Then shall the lame man leap as an hart, and the tongue of

the dumb sing: for in the wilderness shall waters break out, and streams in the desert.

Isaiah 35:7-10:

And the parched ground shall become a pool, and the thirsty land springs of water: in the habitation of dragons, where each lay, shall be grass with reeds and rushes.

And an highway shall be there, and a way, and it shall be called the way of holiness; the unclean shall not pass over it; but it shall be for those: the wayfaring men, though fools, shall not err therein.

No lion shall be there, nor any ravenous beast shall go up thereon, it shall not be found there; but the redeemed shall walk there:

And the ransomed of the Lord shall return, and come to Zion with songs and everlasting joy upon their heads: they shall obtain joy and gladness, and sorrow and sighing shall flee away.

Isaiah 49:6:

And he said, It is a light thing that thou shouldest be my servant to raise up the tribes of Jacob, and to RESTORE the preserved of ISRAEL: I will also give thee for a light to the Gentiles, that thou mayest be my salvation unto the end of the earth.

Isaiah 49:13-16:

Sing, O heavens; and be joyful, O earth; and break forth into singing, O mountains: for the Lord hath comforted his people, and will have mercy upon his afflicted.

But Zion said, The Lord hath forsaken me, and my Lord hath forgotten me.

Can a woman forget her sucking child, that she should not have compassion on the son of her womb? yea, they may forget, yet will I not forget thee.

Behold, I have graven thee upon the palms of my hands; thy walls are continually before me.

Isaiah 49:17-21:

Thy children shall make haste; thy destroyers and they that made thee waste shall go forth of thee.

Lift up thine eyes round about, and behold: all these gather themselves together, and come to thee. As I live, saith the Lord, thou shalt surely clothe thee with them all, as with an ornament, and bind them on thee, as a bride doeth.

For thy waste and thy desolate places, and the land of thy destruction, shall even now be too narrow by reason of the inhabitants, and they that swallowed thee up shall be far away.

The children which thou shalt have, after thou hast lost the other, shall say again in thine ears, The place is too strait for me: give place to me that I may dwell.

Then shalt thou say in thine heart, Who hath begotten me these, seeing I have lost my children, and am desolate, a captive, and removing to and fro? and who hath brought up these? behold, I was left alone; these, where had they been?

Isaiah 49:22-23:

Thus saith the Lord God, Behold, I will lift up mine hand to the Gentiles, and set up my standard to the people: and they shall bring thy sons in their arms, and thy daughters shall be carried upon their shoulders.

And kings shall be thy nursing fathers, and their queens thy nursing mothers: they shall bow down to thee with their face toward the earth, and lick up the dust of thy feet; and thou shalt know that I am the Lord: for they shall not be ashamed that wait for me.

Isaiah 51:3:

For the Lord shall comfort Zion: he will comfort all her waste places; and he will make her wilderness like Eden, and her desert like the garden of the Lord; joy and gladness shall be found therein, thanksgiving, and the voice of melody.

Isaiah 51:11:

Therefore the redeemed of the Lord shall return, and come with singing unto Zion; and everlasting joy shall be upon their head: they shall obtain gladness and joy; and sorrow and mourning shall flee away.

Isaiah 60:1:

Arise, shine; for thy light is come, and the glory of the Lord is risen upon thee.

Isaiah 62:2-3:

And the Gentiles shall see thy righteousness, and all kings thy glory: and thou shalt be called by a new name, which the mouth of the Lord shall name.

Thou shalt also be a crown of glory in the hand of the Lord, and a royal diadem in the hand of thy God.

Isaiah 66:11:

That ye may suck, and be satisfied with the breasts of her consolations; that ye may milk out, and be delighted with the abundance of her glory.

Isaiah 66:14:

And when ye see this, your heart shall rejoice, and your bones shall flourish like an herb: and the hand of the Lord shall be known toward his servants, and his indignation toward his enemies.

Jeremiah 24:6-7:

For I will set mine eyes upon them for good, and I will bring them again to this land: and I will build them, and not pull them down; and I will plant them, and not pluck them up.

And I will give them an heart to know me, that I am the Lord: and they shall be my people, and I will be their God: for they shall return unto me with their whole heart.

Jeremiah 27:22:

They shall be carried to Babylon, and there shall they be until the day that I visit them, saith the Lord; then will I bring them up, and RESTORE them to this place.

Jeremiah 30:3:

For, lo, the days come, saith the Lord, that I will bring again the captivity of my people ISRAEL and Judah, saith the Lord: and I will cause them to return to the land that I gave to their fathers, and they shall possess it.

Jeremiah 30:10-12:

But they shall serve the Lord their God, and David their king, whom I will raise up unto them.

Therefore fear thou not, O my servant Jacob, saith the Lord; neither be dismayed, O ISRAEL: for, lo, I will save thee from afar, and thy seed from the land of their captivity; and Jacob shall return, and shall be in rest, and be quiet, and none shall make him afraid.

For I am with thee, saith the Lord, to save thee:

Jeremiah 30:18:

Thus saith the Lord; Behold, I will bring again the captivity of Jacob's tents, and have mercy on his dwellingplaces; and the city shall be builded upon her own heap, and the palace shall remain after the manner thereof.

Jeremiah 32:37:

Behold, I will gather them out of all countries, whither I have driven them in mine anger, and in my fury, and in great wrath; and I will bring them again unto this place, and I will cause them to dwell safely:

Jeremiah 32:41 & 44:

Yea, I will rejoice over them to do them good, and I will plant them in this land assuredly with my whole heart and with my whole soul.

Men shall buy fields for money, and subscribe evidences, and seal them, and take witnesses in the land of Benjamin, and in the places about Jerusalem, and in the cities of Judah, and in the cities of the mountains, and in the cities of the valley, and in the cities of the south: for I will cause their captivity to return, saith the Lord.

Jeremiah 33:6-7:

Behold, I will bring it health and cure, and I will cure them and will reveal unto them the abundance of peace and truth.

And I will cause the captivity of Judah and the captivity of ISRAEL to return, and will build them, as at the first.

Jeremiah 33:12:

Thus saith the Lord of hosts; Again in this place, which is desolate without man and without beast, and in all the cities thereof, shall be an habitation of shepherds causing their flocks to lie down.

Ezekiel 16:60:

Nevertheless I will remember my covenant with thee in the days of thy youth, and I will establish unto thee an everlasting covenant.

Ezekiel 20:40-41:

For in mine holy mountain, in the mountain of the height of ISRAEL, saith the Lord God, there shall all the house of IS-RAEL, all of them in the land, serve me: there will I accept them, and there will I require your offerings, and the firstfruits of your oblations, with all your holy things.

I will accept you with your sweet savour, when I bring you out from the people, and gather you out of the countries wherein ye have been scattered; and I will be sanctified in you before the heathen.

Ezekiel 36:8-9:

But ye, O mountains of ISRAEL, ye shall shoot forth your branches, and yield your fruit to my people of ISRAEL; for they are at hand to come.

For, behold, I am for you, and I will turn unto you, and ye shall be tilled and sown:

Ezekiel 36:10-12:

And I will multiply men upon you, all the house of IS-RAEL, even all of it: and the cities shall be inhabited, and the wastes shall be builded:

And I will multiply upon you man and beast; and they shall increase and bring fruit: and I will settle you after your old estates, and will do better unto you than at your beginnings: and ye shall know that I am the Lord.

Yea, I will cause men to walk upon you, even my people ISRAEL; and they shall possess thee, and thou shalt be their inheritance, and thou shalt no more henceforth bereave them of men.

Ezekiel 36:23-24:

And I will sanctify my great name, which was profaned among the heathen, which ye have profaned in the midst of them; and the heathen shall know that I am the Lord, saith the Lord God, when I shall be sanctified in you before their eyes.

For I will take you from among the heathen, and gather

you out of all countries, and will bring you into your own land.

Ezekiel 36:25-27:

Then will I sprinkle clean water upon you, and ye shall be clean: from all your filthiness, and from all your idols, will I cleanse you.

A new heart also will I give you, and a new spirit will I put within you: and I will take away the stony heart out of your flesh, and I will give you an heart of flesh.

And I will put my spirit within you, and cause you to walk in my statutes, and ye shall keep my judgments, and do them.

Ezekiel 36:28-30:

And ye shall dwell in the land that I gave to your fathers; and ye shall be My people, and I will be your God.

I will also save you from all your uncleannesses: and I will call for the corn, and will increase it, and lay no famine upon you.

And I will multiply the fruit of the tree, and the increase of the field, that ye shall receive no more reproach of famine among the heathen.

Ezekiel 36:33-36:

Thus saith the Lord God; In the day that I shall have cleansed you from all your iniquities I will also cause you to dwell in the cities, and the wastes shall be builded.

And the desolate land shall be tilled, whereas it lay desolate in the sight of all that passed by.

And they shall say, This land that was desolate is become like the garden of Eden; and the waste and desolate and ruined cities are become fenced, and are inhabited.

Then the heathen that are left round about you shall know that I the Lord build the ruined places, and plant that that was desolate: I the Lord have spoken it, and I will do it.

Ezekiel 36:37-38:

Thus saith the Lord God; I will yet for this be inquired of by the house of ISRAEL, to do it for them; I will increase them with men like a flock.

As the holy flock, as the flock of Jerusalem in her solemn feasts; so shall the waste cities be filled with flocks of men: and they shall know that I am the Lord.

Ezekiel 37:10-11:

So I prophesied as he commanded me, and the breath came into them, and they lived, and stood up upon their feet, an exceeding great army.

Then he said unto me, Son of man, these bones are the whole house of ISRAEL: behold, they say, Our bones are dried, and our hope is lost: we are cut off for our parts.

Ezekiel 37:12-14:

Therefore prophesy and say unto them, Thus saith the Lord God; Behold, O my people, I will open your graves, and cause you to come up out of your graves, and bring you into the land of ISRAEL.

And ye shall know that I am the Lord, when I have opened

your graves, O My people, and brought you up out of your graves,

And shall put my spirit in you, and ye shall live, and I shall place you in your own land: then shall ye know that I the Lord have spoken it, and performed it, saith the Lord.

Ezekiel 37:15-18:

The word of the Lord came again unto me, saying,

Moreover, thou son of man, take thee one stick, and write upon it, For Judah, and for the children of ISRAEL his companions: then take another stick, and write upon it, For Joseph, the stick of Ephraim and for all the house of ISRAEL his companions:

And join them one to another into one stick; and they shall become one in thine hand.

And when the children of thy people shall speak unto thee, saying, Wilt thou not shew us what thou meanest by these?

Ezekiel 37:21-23:

And say unto them, Thus saith the Lord God; Behold, I will take the children of ISRAEL from among the heathen, whither they be gone, and will gather them on every side, and bring them into their own land:

And I will make them one nation in the land upon the mountains of ISRAEL; and one king shall be king to them all: and they shall be no more two nations, neither shall they be divided into two kingdoms any more at all.

Neither shall they defile themselves any more with their idols, nor with their detestable things, nor with any of their transgressions: but I will save them out of all their dwellingplaces, wherein they have sinned, and will cleanse them: so shall they be my people, and I will be their God.

Ezekiel 37:24-25:

And David my servant shall be king over them; and they all shall have one shepherd: they shall also walk in my judgments, and observe my statutes, and do them.

And they shall dwell in the land that I have given unto Jacob my servant, wherein your fathers have dwelt; and they shall dwell therein, even they, and their children, and their children's children for ever: and my servant David shall be their prince for ever.

Ezekiel 37:26-28:

Moreover I will make a covenant of peace with them; it shall be an everlasting covenant with them: and I will place them, and multiply them, and will set my sanctuary in the midst of them for evermore.

My tabernacle also shall be with them: yea, I will be their God, and they shall be my people.

And the heathen shall know that I the Lord do sanctify ISRAEL, when my sanctuary shall be in the midst of them for evermore.

Joel 2:25-27:

And I will RESTORE to you the years that the locust hath eaten, the cankerworm, and the caterpiller, and the palmerworm, my great army which I sent among you.

And ye shall eat in plenty, and be satisfied, and praise the name of the Lord your God, that hath dealt wondrously with you: and my people shall never be ashamed.

And ye shall know that I am in the midst of ISRAEL, and that I am the Lord your God, and none else: and my people shall never be ashamed.

Haggai 2:3-9:

Who is left among you that saw this house in her first glory? and how do ye see it now? is it not in your eyes in comparison of it as nothing?

Yet now be strong, O Zerubbabel, saith the Lord; and be strong, O Joshua, son of Josedech, the high priest; and be strong, all ye people of the land, saith the Lord, and work: for I am with you, saith the Lord of hosts:

According to the word that I covenanted with you when ye came out of Egypt, so my spirit remaineth among you: fear ye not.

For thus saith the Lord of hosts; Yet once, it is a little while, and I will shake the heavens, and the earth, and the sea, and the dry land;

And I will shake all nations, and the desire of all nations shall come: and I will fill this house with glory, saith the Lord of hosts.

The silver is mine, and the gold is mine, saith the Lord of hosts.

The glory of this latter house shall be greater than of the former, saith the Lord of hosts: and in this place will I give peace, saith the Lord of hosts.

Micah 5:3:

Therefore will he give them up, until the time that she which travaileth hath brought forth: then the remnant of his brethren shall return unto the children of ISRAEL.

Zephaniah 2:7:
And the coast shall be for the remnant of the house of Judah; they shall feed thereupon: in the houses of Ashkelon shall they lie down in the evening: for the Lord their God shall visit them, and turn away their captivity.

Zechariah 1:17:
Cry yet, saying, Thus saith the Lord of hosts; My cities through prosperity shall yet be spread abroad; and the Lord shall yet comfort Zion, and shall yet choose Jerusalem.

Zechariah 8:1-3:
Again the word of the Lord of hosts came to me, saying,

Thus saith the Lord of hosts; I was jealous for Zion with great jealousy, and I was jealous for her with great fury.

Thus saith the Lord; I am returned unto Zion, and will dwell in the midst of Jerusalem: and Jerusalem shall be called a city of truth; and the mountain of the Lord of hosts the holy mountain.

Zechariah 8:7-8:
Thus saith the Lord of hosts; Behold, I will save my people from the east country, and from the west country;

And I will bring them, and they shall dwell in the midst of Jerusalem: and they shall be my people, and I will be their God, in truth and in righteousness.

Zechariah 8:12-13:

For the seed shall be prosperous; the vine shall give her fruit, and the ground shall give her increase, and the heavens shall give their dew; and I will cāuse the remnant of this people to possess all these things.

And it shall come to pass, that as ye were a curse among the heathen, O house of Judah, and house of ISRAEL; so will I save you, and ye shall be a blessing: fear not, but let your hands be strong.

Zechariah 8:16:

So again have I thought in these days to do well unto Jerusalem and to the house of Judah: fear ye not.

Zechariah 10:6:

And I will strengthen the house of Judah, and I will save the house of Joseph, and I will bring them again to place them; for I have mercy upon them: and they shall be as though I had not cast them off: for I am the Lord their God, and will hear them.

Zechariah 10:10:

I will bring them again also out of the land of Egypt, and gather them out of Assyria; and I will bring them into the land of Gilead and Lebanon; and place shall not be found for them.

2 Corinthians 3:16:

Nevertheless when it shall turn to the Lord, the vail shall be taken away.

Revelation 7:4-8:

And I heard the number of them which were sealed: and there were sealed an hundred and forty and four thousand of all the tribes of the children of ISRAEL.

Of the tribe of Juda were sealed twelve thousand. Of the tribe of Reuben were sealed twelve thousand. Of the tribe of Gad were sealed twelve thousand.

Of the tribe of Aser were sealed twelve thousand. Of the tribe of Nephthalim were sealed twelve thousand. Of the tribe of Manasses were sealed twelve thousand.

Of the tribe of Simeon were sealed twelve thousand. Of the tribe of Levi were sealed twelve thousand. Of the tribe of Issachar were sealed twelve thousand.

Of the tribe of Zabulon were sealed twelve thousand. Of the tribe of Joseph were sealed twelve thousand. Of the tribe of Benjamin were sealed twelve thousand.

ISRAEL: The Eternal Destiny of the Nation Under Messiah's Rule

Numbers 24:17 & 19:

I shall see him, but not now: I shall behold him, but not nigh: there shall come a Star out of Jacob, and a Sceptre shall rise out of ISRAEL

Out of Jacob shall come he that shall have dominion.

Isaiah 9:6-7:

For unto us a child is born, unto us a son is given: and the government shall be upon his shoulder: and his name shall be called Wonderful, Counsellor, The mighty God, the everlasting Father, The Prince of Peace.

Of the increase of his government and peace there shall be no end, upon the throne of David, and upon his kingdom, to order it, and to establish it with judgment and with justice from henceforth even for ever. The zeal of the Lord of hosts will perform this.

Isaiah 11:1-3:

And there shall come forth a rod out of the stem of Jesse, and a Branch shall grow out of his roots:

And the spirit of the Lord shall rest upon him, the spirit of wisdom and understanding, the spirit of counsel and might, the spirit of knowledge and of the fear of the Lord;

And shall make him of quick understanding in the fear of the Lord: and he shall not judge after the sight of his eyes, neither reprove after the hearing of his ears:

Isaiah 11:10-12:

And in that day there shall be a root of Jesse, which shall stand for an ensign of the people; to it shall the Gentiles seek: and his rest shall be glorious.

And it shall come to pass in that day, that the Lord shall set his hand again the second time to recover the remnant of his people.

And he shall set up an ensign for the nations, and shall assemble the outcasts of ISRAEL, and gather together the dispersed of Judah from the four corners of the earth.

Isaiah 11:16:

And there shall be an highway for the remnant of his people ... like as it was to ISRAEL in the day that he came up out of the land of Egypt.

Isaiah 12:1-5:

And in that day thou shalt say, O Lord, I will praise thee: though thou wast angry with me, thine anger is turned away, and thou comfortedst me.

Behold, God is my salvation; I will trust, and not be afraid: for the Lord Jehovah is my strength and my song; he also is become my salvation.

Therefore with joy shall ye draw water out of the wells of salvation.

And in that day shall ye say, Praise the Lord, call upon his name, declare his doings among the people, make mention that his name is exalted.

Sing unto the Lord; for he hath done excellent things: this is known in all the earth.

Isaiah 28:5:

In that day shall the Lord of hosts be for a crown of glory, and for a diadem of beauty, unto the residue of his people,

Isaiah 55:4-5:

Behold, I have given him for a witness to the people, a leader and commander to the people.

Behold, thou shalt call a nation that thou knowest not, and nations that knew not thee shall run unto thee because of the Lord thy God, and for the Holy One of Israel; for he hath glorified thee.

Isaiah 59:20-21:

And the Redeemer shall come to Zion, and unto them that turn from transgression in Jacob, saith the Lord.

As for me, this is my covenant with them, saith the Lord; My spirit that is upon thee, and my words which I have put in thy mouth, shall not depart out of thy mouth, nor out of the mouth of thy seed, nor out of the mouth of thy seed's seed, saith the Lord, from henceforth and for ever.

Daniel 7:13-14:

I saw in the night visions, and, behold, one like the Son of man came with the clouds of heaven, and came to the Ancient of days, and they brought him near before him.

And there was given him dominion, and glory, and a kingdom, that all people, nations, and languages, should serve him: his dominion is an everlasting dominion, which shall not pass away, and his kingdom that which shall not be destroyed.

Daniel 2:44-45:

And in the days of these kings shall the God of heaven set up a kingdom, which shall never be destroyed: and the kingdom shall not be left to other people, but it shall break in pieces and consume all these kingdoms, and it shall stand for ever.

Forasmuch as thou sawest that the stone was cut out of the mountain without hands, and that it brake in pieces the iron, the brass, the clay, the silver, and the gold; the great God hath made known to the king what shall come to pass hereafter: and the dream is certain, and the interpretation thereof sure.

Daniel 7:13-14:

I saw in the night visions, and, behold, one like the Son of man came with the clouds of heaven, and came to the Ancient of days, and they brought him near before him.

And there was given him dominion, and glory, and a kingdom, that all people, nations, and languages, should serve him: his dominion is an everlasting dominion, which shall not pass away, and his kingdom that which shall not be destroyed.

Daniel 7:27:

And the kingdom and dominion, and the greatness of the kingdom under the whole heaven, shall be given to the people of the saints of the most High, whose kingdom is an everlasting kingdom, and all dominions shall serve and obey him.

Hosea 3:4-5:

For the children of Israel shall abide many days without a king, and without a prince, and without a sacrifice, and without an image, and without an ephod, and without teraphim:

Afterward shall the children of Israel return, and seek the Lord their God, and David their king; and shall fear the Lord and his goodness in the latter days.

Micah 5:2:

But thou, Bethlehem Ephratah, though thou be little among the thousands of Judah, yet out of thee shall he come forth unto me that is to be ruler in Israel; whose goings forth have been from of old, from everlasting.

Zechariah 9:9-10:

Rejoice greatly, O daughter of Zion; shout, O daughter of Jerusalem: behold, thy King cometh unto thee: he is just, and having salvation; lowly, and riding upon an ass, and upon a colt the foal of an ass.

And I will cut off the chariot from Ephraim, and the horse from Jerusalem, and the battle bow shall be cut off: and he shall speak peace unto the heathen: and his dominion shall be from sea even to sea, and from the river even to the ends of the earth.

Zechariah 14:9:

And the Lord shall be king over all the earth: in that day shall there be one Lord, and his name one.

Malachi 3:1-3:

Behold, I will send my messenger, and he shall prepare the way before me: and the Lord, whom ye seek, shall suddenly come to his temple, even the messenger of the covenant, whom ye delight in: behold, he shall come, saith the Lord of hosts.

But who may abide the day of his coming? and who shall stand when he appeareth? for he is like a refiner's fire, and like fullers' soap:

And he shall sit as a refiner and purifier of silver: and he shall purify the sons of Levi, and purge them as gold and silver, that they may offer unto the Lord an offering in righteousness.

Luke 1:32-33:

He shall be great, and shall be called the Son of the Highest: and the Lord God shall give unto him the throne of his father David:

And he shall reign over the house of Jacob for ever; and of his kingdom there shall be no end.

Revelation 5:10:

And hast made us unto our God kings and priests: and we shall reign on the earth.

Revelation 11:15:

And the seventh angel sounded; and there were great voices in heaven, saying, The kingdoms of this world are become the kingdoms of our Lord, and of his Christ; and he shall reign for ever and ever.

Revelation 20:4-6:

And I saw thrones, and they sat upon them, and judgment was given unto them: ... and they lived and reigned with Christ a thousand years.

But the rest of the dead lived not again until the thousand years were finished. This is the first resurrection.

Blessed and holy is he that hath part in the first resurrection: on such the second death hath no power, but they shall be priests of God and of Christ, and shall reign with him a thousand years.

Revelation 21:1-5:

And I saw a new heaven and a new earth: for the first heaven and the first earth were passed away; and there was no more sea.

And I John saw the holy city, new JERUSALEM, coming down from God out of heaven, prepared as a bride adorned for her husband.

And I heard a great voice out of heaven saying, Behold, the tabernacle of God is with men, and he will dwell with them, and they shall be his people, and God himself shall be with them, and be their God.

And God shall wipe away all tears from their eyes; and there shall be no more death, neither sorrow, nor crying, neither shall there be any more pain: for the former things are passed away.

And he that sat upon the throne said, Behold, I make all things new. And he said unto me, Write: for these words are true and faithful.

Revelation 21:22-27:

And I saw no temple therein: for the Lord God Almighty and the Lamb are the temple of it.

And the city had no need of the sun, neither of the moon, to shine in it: for the glory of God did lighten it, and the Lamb is the light thereof.

And the nations of them which are saved shall walk in the light of it: and the kings of the earth do bring their glory and honour into it.

And the gates of it shall not be shut at all by day: for there shall be no night there.

And they shall bring the glory and honour of the nations into it.

And there shall in no wise enter into it any thing that defileth, neither whatsoever worketh abomination, or maketh a lie: but they which are written in the Lamb's book of life.

Revelation 22:1-5:

And he shewed me a pure river of water of life, clear as crystal, proceeding out of the throne of God and of the Lamb.

In the midst of the street of it, and on either side of the river, was there the tree of life, which bare twelve manner of fruits, and yielded her fruit every month: and the leaves of the tree were for the healing of the nations.

And there shall be no more curse: but the throne of God and of the Lamb shall be in it; and his servants shall serve him:

And they shall see his face; and his name shall be in their foreheads.

And there shall be no night there; and they need no candle, neither light of the sun; for the Lord God giveth them light: and they shall reign for ever and ever.

The Nations

Isaiah 66:18-20:

For I know their works and their thoughts: it shall come, that I will gather ALL NATIONS and tongues; and they shall come, and see my glory.

And I will set a sign among them, and I will send those that escape of them unto THE NATIONS, to Tarshish, Pul, and Lud, that draw the bow, to Tubal, and Javan, to the isles afar off, that have not heard my fame, neither have seen my glory; and they shall declare my glory among the Gentiles [THE NATIONS].

And they shall bring all your brethren for an offering unto the Lord out of all NATIONS upon horses, and in chariots, and in litters, and upon mules, and upon swift beasts, to my holy mountain Jerusalem, saith the Lord, as the children of Israel bring an offering in a clean vessel into the house of the Lord.

The Ingathering From
THE NATIONS

Genesis 49:10:

The sceptre shall not depart from Judah, nor a lawgiver from between his feet, until Shiloh come; and unto him shall the gathering of the people be.

Deuteronomy 29:16:

(For ye know how we have dwelt in the land of Egypt; and how we came through THE NATIONS which ye passed by;

Deuteronomy 30:3:

That then the Lord thy God will turn thy captivity, and have compassion upon thee, and will return and gather thee from all THE NATIONS, whither the Lord thy God hath scattered thee.

Isaiah 11:11-12:

And it shall come to pass in that day, that the Lord shall set his hand again the second time to recover the remnant of his people, which shall be left, from Assyria, and from Egypt, and from Pathros, and from Cush, and from Elam, and from Shinar, and from Hamath, and from the islands of the sea.

And he shall set up an ensign for THE NATIONS, and shall assemble the outcasts of Israel, and gather together the dispersed of Judah from the four corners of the earth.

Isaiah 27:13:

And it shall come to pass in that day, that the great trumpet shall be blown, and they shall come which were ready to perish in the land of Assyria, and the outcasts in the land of Egypt, and shall worship the Lord in the holy mount at Jerusalem.

Isaiah 49:22-23:

Thus saith the Lord God, Behold, I will lift up mine hand to the Gentiles [THE NATIONS], and set up my standard to the people: and they shall bring thy sons in their arms, and thy daughters shall be carried upon their shoulders.

And kings shall be thy nursing fathers, and their queens thy nursing mothers: they shall bow down to thee with their face toward the earth, and lick up the dust of thy feet; and thou shalt know that I am the Lord: for they shall not be ashamed that wait for me.

Isaiah 51:11:

Therefore the redeemed of the Lord shall return, and come with singing unto Zion; and everlasting joy shall be upon their head: they shall obtain gladness and joy; and sorrow and mourning shall flee away.

Isaiah 66:8:

Who hath heard such a thing? who hath seen such things? Shall the earth be made to bring forth in one day? or shall a nation be born at once? for as soon as Zion travailed, she brought forth her children.

Jeremiah 3:14:

Turn, O backsliding children, saith the Lord; for I am married unto you: and I will take you one of a city, and two of a family, and I will bring you to Zion:

Jeremiah 12:14-16:

Thus saith the Lord against all mine evil neighbours, that touch the inheritance which I have caused my people Israel to inherit; Behold, I will pluck them out of their land, and pluck out the house of Judah from among them.

And it shall come to pass, after that I have plucked them out I will return, and have compassion on them, and will bring them again, every man to his heritage, and every man to his land.

And it shall come to pass, if they will diligently learn the ways of my people, to swear by my name, The Lord liveth; as they taught my people to swear by Baal; then shall they be built in the midst of my people.

Jeremiah 16:14-15:

Therefore, behold, the days come, saith the Lord, that it shall no more be said, The Lord liveth, that brought up the children of Israel out of the land of Egypt;

But, The Lord liveth, that brought up the children of Israel from the land of the north, and from all the lands whither he had driven them: and I will bring them again into their land that I gave unto their fathers.

Jeremiah 23:3:

And I will gather the remnant of my flock out of all countries whither I have driven them, and will bring them again to their folds; and they shall be fruitful and increase.

Jeremiah 29:14:

And I will be found of you, saith the Lord: and I will turn away your captivity, and I will gather you from all THE NATIONS, and from all the places whither I have driven you, saith the Lord; and I will bring you again into the place whence I caused you to be carried away captive.

Jeremiah 31:10:

Hear the word of the Lord, O ye NATIONS, and declare it in the isles afar off, and say, He that scattered Israel will gather him, and keep him, as a shepherd doth his flock.

Jeremiah 33:19-26:

And the word of the Lord came unto Jeremiah, saying,

Thus saith the Lord; If ye can break my covenant of the day, and my covenant of the night, and that there should not be day and night in their season;

Then may also my covenant be broken with David my servant, that he should not have a son to reign upon his throne; and with the Levites the priests, my ministers.

As the host of heaven cannot be numbered, neither the

sand of the sea measured: so will I multiply the seed of David my servant, and the Levites that minister unto me.

Moreover the word of the Lord came to Jeremiah, saying,

Considerest thou not what this people have spoken, saying, The two families which the Lord hath chosen, he hath even cast them off? thus they have despised my people, that they should be no more a nation before them.

Thus saith the Lord; If my covenant be not with day and night, and if I have not appointed the ordinances of heaven and earth;

Then will I cast away the seed of Jacob and David my servant, so that I will not take any of his seed to be rulers over the seed of Abraham, Isaac, and Jacob: for I will cause their captivity to return, and have mercy on them.

Jeremiah 43:5:

But Johanan the son of Kareah, and all the captains of the forces, took all the remnant of Judah, that were returned from all NATIONS, whither they had been driven, to dwell in the land of Judah;

Ezekiel 20:33-36:

As I live, saith the Lord God, surely with a mighty hand, and with a stretched out arm, and with fury poured out, will I rule over you:

And I will bring you out from the people, and will gather you out of the countries wherein ye are scattered, with a mighty hand, and with a stretched out arm, and with fury poured out.

And I will bring you into the wilderness of the people, and there will I plead with you face to face.

Like as I pleaded with your fathers in the wilderness of the land of Egypt, so will I plead with you, saith the Lord God.

Ezekiel 38:8:

After many days thou shalt be visited: in the latter years thou shalt come into the land that is brought back from the sword, and is gathered out of many people, against the mountains of Israel, which have been always waste: but it is brought forth out of THE NATIONS, and they shall dwell safely all of them.

Jeremiah 50:5:

They shall ask the way to Zion with their faces thitherward, saying, Come, and let us join ourselves to the Lord in a perpetual covenant that shall not be forgotten.

Ezekiel 38:12:

To take a spoil, and to take a prey; to turn thine hand upon the desolate places that are now inhabited, and upon the people that are gathered out of THE NATIONS, which have gotten cattle and goods, that dwell in the midst of the land.

Hosea 8:10:

Yea, though they have hired among THE NATIONS, now will I gather them, and they shall sorrow a little for the burden of the king of princes.

Joel 3:2:

I will also gather all NATIONS, and will bring them down

into the valley of Jehoshaphat, and will plead with them there for my people and for my heritage Israel, whom they have scattered among THE NATIONS, and parted my land.

Zephaniah 3:20:

At that time will I bring you again, even in the time that I gather you: for I will make you a name and a praise among all people of the earth, when I turn back your captivity before your eyes, saith the Lord.

Zechariah 8:8:

And I will bring them, and they shall dwell in the midst of Jerusalem: and they shall be my people, and I will be their God, in truth and in righteousness.

Zechariah 9:11-12:

As for thee also, by the blood of thy covenant I have sent forth thy prisoners out of the pit wherein is no water.

Turn you to the strong hold, ye prisoners of hope: even to day do I declare that I will render double unto thee;

Zechariah 10:10:

I will bring them again also out of the land of Egypt, and gather them out of Assyria; and I will bring them into the land of Gilead and Lebanon; and place shall not be found for them.

The Gathering of
THE NATIONS to Zion

Psalms 22:27-28:

All the ends of the world shall remember and turn unto the Lord: and all the kindreds of THE NATIONS shall worship before thee.

For the kingdom is the Lord's: and he is the governor among THE NATIONS.

Psalms 86:9:

All NATIONS whom thou hast made shall come and worship before thee, O Lord; and shall glorify thy name.

Isaiah 2:2-3:

And it shall come to pass in the last days, that the mountain of the Lord's house shall be established in the top of the mountains, and shall be exalted above the hills; and all NATIONS shall flow unto it.

And many people shall go and say, Come ye, and let us go up to the mountain of the Lord, to the house of the God of

Jacob; and he will teach us of his ways, and we will walk in his paths: for out of Zion shall go forth the law, and the word of the Lord from Jerusalem.

Isaiah 5:26:

And he will lift up an ensign to THE NATIONS from far, and will hiss unto them from the end of the earth: and, behold, they shall come with speed swiftly:

Isaiah 11:10:

And in that day there shall be a root of Jesse, which shall stand for an ensign of the people; to it shall the Gentiles [THE NATIONS] seek: and his rest shall be glorious.

Isaiah 43:9:

Let all THE NATIONS be gathered together, and let the people be assembled: who among them can declare this, and shew us former things? let them bring forth their witnesses, that they may be justified: or let them hear, and say, It is truth.

Isaiah 45:20:

Assemble yourselves and come; draw near together, ye that are escaped of THE NATIONS:

Isaiah 55:5:

Behold, thou shalt call a nation that thou knowest not, and NATIONS that knew not thee shall run unto thee because of the Lord thy God, and for the Holy One of Israel; for he hath glorified thee.

Isaiah 60:1-3:

Arise, shine; for thy light is come, and the glory of the Lord is risen upon thee.

For, behold, the darkness shall cover the earth, and gross darkness the people: but the Lord shall arise upon thee, and his glory shall be seen upon thee.

And the Gentiles [THE NATIONS] shall come to thy light, and kings to the brightness of thy rising.

Isaiah 60:4-5:

Lift up thine eyes round about, and see: all they gather themselves together, they come to thee: thy sons shall come from far, and thy daughters shall be nursed at thy side.

Then thou shalt see, and flow together, and thine heart shall fear, and be enlarged; because the abundance of the sea shall be converted unto thee, the forces of the Gentiles [THE NATIONS] shall come unto thee.

Isaiah 66:18:

For I know their works and their thoughts: it shall come, that I will gather all NATIONS and tongues; and they shall come, and see my glory.

Jeremiah 3:17:

At that time they shall call Jerusalem the throne of the Lord; and all THE NATIONS shall be gathered unto it, to the name of the Lord, to Jerusalem: neither shall they walk any more after the imagination of their evil heart.

Jeremiah 16:19:

O Lord, my strength, and my fortress, and my refuge in

the day of affliction, the Gentiles [THE NATIONS] shall come unto thee from the ends of the earth, and shall say, Surely our fathers have inherited lies, vanity, and things wherein there is no profit.

Joel 3:12:

Let the heathen [THE NATIONS] be wakened, and come up to the valley of Jehoshaphat: for there will I sit to judge all the heathen [THE NATIONS] round about.

Micah 4:2-3:

And many NATIONS shall come, and say, Come, and let us go up to the mountain of the Lord, and to the house of the God of Jacob; and he will teach us of his ways, and we will walk in his paths: for the law shall go forth of Zion, and the word of the Lord from Jerusalem.

And he shall judge among many people, and rebuke strong NATIONS afar off; and they shall beat their swords into plowshares, and their spears into pruninghooks: nation shall not lift up a sword against nation, neither shall they learn war any more.

Zephaniah 3:8:

Therefore wait ye upon me, saith the Lord, until the day that I rise up to the prey: for my determination is to gather THE NATIONS, that I may assemble the kingdoms.

Haggai 2:7:

And I will shake all NATIONS, and the desire of all NA-

TIONS shall come: and I will fill this house with glory, saith the Lord of hosts.

Zechariah 8:22-23:

Yea, many people and strong NATIONS shall come to seek the Lord of hosts in Jerusalem, and to pray before the Lord.

Thus saith the Lord of hosts; In those days it shall come to pass, that ten men shall take hold out of all languages of THE NATIONS, even shall take hold of the skirt of him that is a Jew, saying, We will go with you: for we have heard that God is with you.

Mark 11:17:

And he taught, saying unto them, Is it not written, My house shall be called of all NATIONS the house of prayer?

Revelation 7:9:

After this I beheld, and, lo, a great multitude, which no man could number, of all NATIONS, and kindreds, and people, and tongues, stood before the throne, and before the Lamb, clothed with white robes, and palms in their hands;

Revelation 15:4:

Who shall not fear thee, O Lord, and glorify thy name? for thou only art holy: for all NATIONS shall come and worship before thee; for thy judgments are made manifest.

Revelation 21:24:

And THE NATIONS of them which are saved shall walk

in the light of it: and the kings of the earth do bring their glory and honour into it.

Revelation 21:26:

And they shall bring the glory and honour of THE NATIONS into it.

The Thrust to THE NATIONS

Deuteronomy 28:37:

And thou shalt become an astonishment, a proverb, and a byword, among all NATIONS whither the Lord shall lead thee.

1 Chronicles 16:31:

Let the heavens be glad, and let the earth rejoice: and let men say among THE NATIONS, The Lord reigneth.

Isaiah 45:1-3:

Thus saith the Lord to his anointed, to Cyrus, whose right hand I have holden, to subdue nations before him; and I will loose the loins of kings, to open before him the two leaved gates; and the gates shall not be shut;

I will go before thee, and make the crooked places straight: I will break in pieces the gates of brass, and cut in sunder the bars of iron:

And I will give thee the treasures of darkness, and hidden riches of secret places, that thou mayest know that I, the Lord, which call thee by thy name, am the God of Israel.

Isaiah 49:6:

And he said, It is a light thing that thou shouldest be my servant to raise up the tribes of Jacob, and to restore the preserved of Israel: I will also give thee for a light to the Gentiles [THE NATIONS], that thou mayest be my salvation unto the end of the earth.

Isaiah 52:10:

The Lord hath made bare his holy arm in the eyes of all THE NATIONS; and all the ends of the earth shall see the salvation of our God.

Isaiah 52:15:

So shall he sprinkle many NATIONS; the kings shall shut their mouths at him: for that which had not been told them shall they see; and that which they had not heard shall they consider.

Isaiah 64:2:

As when the melting fire burneth, the fire causeth the waters to boil, to make thy name known to thine adversaries, that THE NATIONS may tremble at thy presence!

Isaiah 66:19:

And I will set a sign among them, and I will send those that escape of them unto THE NATIONS, to Tarshish, Pul, and Lud, that draw the bow, to Tubal, and Javan, to the isles afar off, that have not heard my fame, neither have seen my glory; and they shall declare my glory among the Gentiles [THE NATIONS].

Jeremiah 1:10:

See, I have this day set thee over THE NATIONS and over the kingdoms, to root out, and to pull down, and to destroy, and to throw down, to build, and to plant.

Jeremiah 4:2:

And thou shalt swear, The Lord liveth, in truth, in judgment, and in righteousness; and THE NATIONS shall bless themselves in him, and in him shall they glory.

Jeremiah 10:7:

Who would not fear thee, O King of NATIONS? for to thee doth it appertain: forasmuch as among all the wise men of THE NATIONS, and in all their kingdoms, there is none like unto thee.

Jeremiah 25:14-15:

For many NATIONS and great kings shall serve themselves of them also: and I will recompense them according to their deeds, and according to the works of their own hands.

For thus saith the Lord God of Israel unto me; Take the wine cup of this fury at my hand, and cause all THE NATIONS, to whom I send thee, to drink it.

Jeremiah 25:17:

Then took I the cup at the Lord's hand, and made all THE NATIONS to drink, unto whom the Lord had sent me:

Jeremiah 25:31:

A noise shall come even to the ends of the earth; for the Lord hath a controversy with THE NATIONS, he will plead with all flesh; he will give them that are wicked to the sword, saith the Lord.

Jeremiah 31:7:

For thus saith the Lord; Sing with gladness for Jacob, and shout among the chief of THE NATIONS: publish ye, praise ye, and say, O Lord, save thy people, the remnant of Israel.

Jeremiah 33:9:

And it shall be to me a name of joy, a praise and an honour before all THE NATIONS of the earth, which shall hear all the good that I do unto them: and they shall fear and tremble for all the goodness and for all the prosperity that I procure unto it.

Ezekiel 38:23:

Thus will I magnify myself, and sanctify myself; and I will be known in the eyes of many NATIONS, and they shall know that I am the Lord.

Zechariah 2:8:

For thus saith the Lord of hosts; After the glory hath he sent me unto THE NATIONS which spoiled you: for he that toucheth you toucheth the apple of his eye.

Zechariah 2:11:

And many NATIONS shall be joined to the Lord in that

day, and shall be my people: and I will dwell in the midst of thee, and thou shalt know that the Lord of hosts hath sent me unto thee.

Matthew 12:21:
And in his name shall the Gentiles [THE NATIONS] trust.

Matthew 24:14:
And this gospel of the kingdom shall be preached in all the world for a witness unto all NATIONS; and then shall the end come.

Matthew 28:19:
Go ye therefore, and teach all NATIONS,

Luke 24:47:
And that repentance and remission of sins should be preached in his name among all NATIONS, beginning at Jerusalem.

Acts 13:47:
For so hath the Lord commanded us, saying, I have set thee to be a light of the Gentiles [THE NATIONS], that thou shouldest be for salvation unto the ends of the earth.

Acts 28:28:
Be it known therefore unto you, that the salvation of God is sent unto the Gentiles [THE NATIONS], and that they will hear it.

Romans 15:12:

And again, Esaias saith, There shall be a root of Jesse, and he that shall rise to reign over the Gentiles [THE NATIONS]; in him shall the Gentiles [THE NATIONS] trust.

Revelation 10:11:

And he said unto me, Thou must prophesy again before many peoples, and NATIONS, and tongues, and kings.

The Offering
From THE NATIONS

2 Samuel 8:11:

Which also king David did dedicate unto the Lord, with the silver and gold that he had dedicated of all NATIONS which he subdued;

2 Chronicles 32:23:

And many brought gifts unto the Lord to Jerusalem, and presents to Hezekiah king of Judah: so that he was magnified in the sight of all NATIONS from thenceforth.

Psalms 68:29:

Because of thy temple at Jerusalem shall kings bring presents unto thee.

Isaiah 18:7:

In that time shall the present be brought unto the Lord of hosts of a people scattered and peeled, and from a people terrible from their beginning hitherto; a nation meted out and trodden under foot, whose land the rivers have spoiled, to the place of the name of the Lord of hosts, the mount Zion.

Isaiah 60:9:

Surely the isles shall wait for me, and the ships of Tarshish first, to bring thy sons from far, their silver and their gold with them, unto the name of the Lord thy God, and to the Holy One of Israel, because he hath glorified thee.

Isaiah 60:11:

Therefore thy gates shall be open continually; they shall not be shut day nor night; that men may bring unto thee the forces of the Gentiles [THE NATIONS], and that their kings may be brought.

Isaiah 66:20:

And they shall bring all your brethren for an offering unto the Lord out of all NATIONS upon horses, and in chariots, and in litters, and upon mules, and upon swift beasts, to my holy mountain Jerusalem, saith the Lord, as the children of Israel bring an offering in a clean vessel into the house of the Lord.

Jeremiah 33:11:

The voice of joy, and the voice of gladness, the voice of the bridegroom, and the voice of the bride, the voice of them that shall say, Praise the Lord of hosts: for the Lord is good; for his mercy endureth for ever: and of them that shall bring the sacrifice of praise into the house of the Lord. For I will cause to return the captivity of the land, as at the first, saith the Lord.

Zephaniah 3:10:

From beyond the rivers of Ethiopia my suppliants, even the daughter of my dispersed, shall bring mine offering.

Zechariah 14:16:

And it shall come to pass, that every one that is left of all THE NATIONS which came against Jerusalem shall even go up from year to year to worship the King, the Lord of hosts, and to keep the feast of tabernacles.

Zechariah 14:19:

This shall be the punishment of Egypt, and the punishment of all NATIONS that come not up to keep the feast of tabernacles.

Malachi 1:11:

For from the rising of the sun even unto the going down of the same my name shall be great among the Gentiles [THE NATIONS]; and in every place incense shall be offered unto my name, and a pure offering: for my name shall be great among the heathen [THE NATIONS], saith the Lord of hosts.

Romans 15:16:

That I should be the minister of Jesus Christ to the Gentiles [THE NATIONS], ministering the gospel of God, that the offering up of the Gentiles [THE NATIONS] might be acceptable, being sanctified by the Holy Ghost.

Romans 15:27:

It hath pleased them verily; and their debtors they are. For if the Gentiles [THE NATIONS] have been made partakers of their spiritual things, their duty is also to minister unto them in carnal things.

Other Significant Verses About THE NATIONS

Genesis 17:16:

And I will bless her, and give thee a son also of her: yea, I will bless her, and she shall be a mother of NATIONS; kings of people shall be of her.

Genesis 18:18:

Seeing that Abraham shall surely become a great and mighty nation, and all THE NATIONS of the earth shall be blessed in him?

Genesis 35:11:

And God said unto him, I am God Almighty: be fruitful and multiply; a nation and a company of NATIONS shall be of thee, and kings shall come out of thy loins;

Genesis 22:18:

And in thy seed shall all THE NATIONS of the earth be blessed; because thou hast obeyed my voice.

Exodus 34:24:

For I will cast out THE NATIONS before thee, and en-large thy borders: neither shall any man desire thy land, when thou shalt go up to appear before the Lord thy God thrice in the year.

Leviticus 18:28:

That the land spue not you out also, when ye defile it, as it spued out THE NATIONS that were before you.

Numbers 14:15:

THE NATIONS ... have heard the fame of thee.

Deuteronomy 4:6:

Keep therefore and do them; for this is your wisdom and your understanding in the sight of THE NATIONS, which shall hear all these statutes, and say, Surely this great nation is a wise and understanding people.

Deuteronomy 4:38:

To drive out NATIONS from before thee greater and mightier than thou art, to bring thee in, to give thee their land for an inheritance, as it is this day.

Deuteronomy 9:4-5:

Speak not thou in thine heart, after that the Lord thy God hath cast them out from before thee, saying, For my right-eousness the Lord hath brought me in to possess this land: but for the wickedness of these NATIONS the Lord doth drive them out from before thee.

Not for thy righteousness, or for the uprightness of thine heart, dost thou go to possess their land: but for the wickedness of these NATIONS the Lord thy God doth drive them out from before thee, and that he may perform the word which the Lord sware unto thy fathers, Abraham, Isaac, and Jacob.

Deuteronomy 11:23:

Then will the Lord drive out all these NATIONS from before you, and ye shall possess greater NATIONS and mightier than yourselves.

Deuteronomy 15:6:

For the Lord thy God blesseth thee, as he promised thee: and thou shalt lend unto many NATIONS, but thou shalt not borrow; and thou shalt reign over many NATIONS, but they shall not reign over thee.

Deuteronomy 32:43:

Rejoice, O ye NATIONS, with his people: for he will avenge the blood of his servants, and will render vengeance to his adversaries, and will be merciful unto his land, and to his people.

Joshua 23:3-4:

And ye have seen all that the Lord your God hath done unto all these NATIONS because of you; for the Lord your God is he that hath fought for you.

Behold, I have divided unto you by lot these NATIONS that remain, to be an inheritance for your tribes, from Jordan, with all THE NATIONS that I have cut off, even unto the great sea westward.

Joshua 23:9:

For the Lord hath driven out from before you great NATIONS and strong: but as for you, no man hath been able to stand before you unto this day.

Judges 2:21:

I also will not henceforth drive out any from before them of THE NATIONS which Joshua left when he died:

Judges 3:1:

Now these are THE NATIONS which the Lord left, to prove Israel by them, even as many of Israel as had not known all the wars of Canaan;

2 Samuel 7:23:

And what one nation in the earth is like thy people, even like Israel, whom God went to redeem for a people to himself, and to make him a name, and to do for you great things and terrible, for thy land, before thy people, which thou redeemedst to thee from Egypt, from THE NATIONS and their gods?

1 Chronicles 17:21:

And what one nation in the earth is like thy people Israel, whom God went to redeem to be his own people, to make thee a name of greatness and terribleness, by driving out

NATIONS from before thy people whom thou hast redeemed out of Egypt?

Psalms 47:3:
He shall subdue the people under us, and THE NATIONS under our feet.

Psalms 67:4:
O let THE NATIONS be glad and sing for joy: for thou shalt judge the people righteously, and govern THE NATIONS upon earth. Selah.

Psalms 72:11:
Yea, all kings shall fall down before him: all NATIONS shall serve him.

Psalms 72:17:
His name shall endure for ever: his name shall be continued as long as the sun: and men shall be blessed in him: all NATIONS shall call him blessed.

Psalms 135:10:
Who smote great NATIONS, and slew mighty kings;

Isaiah 29:7-8:
And the multitude of all THE NATIONS that fight against Ariel, even all that fight against her and her munition, and that distress her, shall be as a dream of a night vision.

It shall even be as when an hungry man dreameth, and, behold, he eateth; but he awaketh, and his soul is empty: or as when a thirsty man dreameth, and, behold, he drinketh; but he awaketh, and, behold, he is faint, and his soul hath appetite: so shall the multitude of all THE NATIONS be, that fight against mount Zion.

Isaiah 41:2:

Who raised up the righteous man from the east, called him to his foot, gave THE NATIONS before him, and made him rule over kings? he gave them as the dust to his sword, and as driven stubble to his bow.

Isaiah 60:16:

Thou shalt also suck the milk of the Gentiles [THE NATIONS], and shalt suck the breast of kings: and thou shalt know that I the Lord am thy Saviour and thy Redeemer, the mighty One of Jacob.

Isaiah 66:12:

For thus saith the Lord, Behold, I will extend peace to her like a river, and the glory of the Gentiles [THE NATIONS] like a flowing stream: then shall ye suck, ye shall be borne upon her sides, and be dandled upon her knees.

Daniel 7:14:

And there was given him dominion, and glory, and a kingdom, that all people, NATIONS, and languages, should serve him: his dominion is an everlasting dominion, which shall not pass away, and his kingdom that which shall not be destroyed.

Micah 5:8:

And the remnant of Jacob shall be among the Gentiles [THE NATIONS] in the midst of many people as a lion among the beasts of the forest, as a young lion among the flocks of sheep: who, if he go through, both treadeth down, and teareth in pieces, and none can deliver.

Habakkuk 3:6:

He stood, and measured the earth: he beheld, and drove asunder THE NATIONS; and the everlasting mountains were scattered, the perpetual hills did bow: his ways are everlasting.

Malachi 3:12:

And all NATIONS shall call you blessed: for ye shall be a delightsome land, saith the Lord of hosts.

Matthew 25:32:

And before him shall be gathered all NATIONS: and he shall separate them one from another, as a shepherd divideth his sheep from the goats:

Luke 2:32:

A light to lighten the Gentiles [THE NATIONS], and the glory of thy people Israel.

Acts 9:15:

But the Lord said unto him, Go thy way: for he is a chosen vessel unto me, to bear my name before the Gentiles [THE NATIONS], and kings, and the children of Israel:

Acts 10:45:

And they of the circumcision which believed were aston-ished, as many as came with Peter, because that on the Gentiles [THE NATIONS] also was poured out the gift of the Holy Ghost.

Acts 11:1:

And the apostles and brethren that were in Judaea heard that the Gentiles [THE NATIONS] had also received the word of God.

Acts 11:18:

When they heard these things, they held their peace, and glorified God, saying, Then hath God also to the Gentiles [THE NATIONS] granted repentance unto life.

Acts 15:7:

And when there had been much disputing, Peter rose up, and said unto them, Men and brethren, ye know how that a good while ago God made choice among us, that the Gentiles [THE NATIONS] by my mouth should hear the word of the gospel, and believe.

Acts 15:12:

Then all the multitude kept silence, and gave audience to Barnabas and Paul, declaring what miracles and wonders God had wrought among the Gentiles [THE NATIONS] by them.

Acts 15:14:

Simeon hath declared how God at the first did visit the

Gentiles [THE NATIONS], to take out of them a people for his name.

Acts 15:17:

That the residue of men might seek after the Lord, and all the Gentiles [THE NATIONS], upon whom my name is called, saith the Lord, who doeth all these things.

Acts 21:19:

And when he had saluted them, he declared particularly what things God had wrought among the Gentiles [THE NATIONS] by his ministry.

Romans 4:17-18:

(As it is written, I have made thee a father of many NATIONS,) before him whom he believed, even God, who quickeneth the dead, and calleth those things which be not as though they were.

Who against hope believed in hope, that he might become the father of many NATIONS; according to that which was spoken, So shall thy seed be.

Romans 15:9:

And that the Gentiles [THE NATIONS] might glorify God for his mercy; as it is written, For this cause I will confess to thee among the Gentiles [THE NATIONS], and sing unto thy name.

Romans 15:27:

It hath pleased them verily; and their debtors they are.

For if the Gentiles [THE NATIONS] have been made partakers of their spiritual things, their duty is also to minister unto them in carnal things.

1 Corinthians 10:32:
Give none offence, neither to the Jews, nor to the Gentiles [THE NATIONS], nor to the church of God:

Galatians 2:2:
And I went up by revelation, and communicated unto them that gospel which I preach among the Gentiles [THE NATIONS], but privately to them which were of reputation, lest by any means I should run, or had run, in vain.

Galatians 3:8:
And the scripture, foreseeing that God would justify the heathen through faith, preached before the gospel unto Abraham, saying, In thee shall all NATIONS be blessed.

Galatians 3:14:
That the blessing of Abraham might come on the Gentiles [THE NATIONS] through Jesus Christ; that we might receive the promise of the Spirit through faith.

Ephesians 3:6:
That the Gentiles [THE NATIONS] should be fellowheirs, and of the same body, and partakers of his promise in Christ by the gospel:

Ephesians 3:8:
Unto me, who am less than the least of all saints, is this

grace given, that I should preach among the Gentiles [THE NATIONS] the unsearchable riches of Christ;

Colossians 1:27:

To whom God would make known what is the riches of the glory of this mystery among the Gentiles [THE NATIONS]; which is Christ in you, the hope of glory:

2 Timothy 4:17:

Notwithstanding the Lord stood with me, and strengthened me; that by me the preaching might be fully known, and that all the Gentiles [THE NATIONS] might hear:

More Lengthy Passages
To Be Considered

Genesis 32:24-30:

And Jacob was left alone; and there wrestled a man with him until the breaking of the day.

And when he saw that he prevailed not against him, he touched the hollow of his thigh; and the hollow of Jacob's thigh was out of joint, as he wrestled with him.

And he said, Let me go, for the day breaketh. And he said, I will not let thee go, except thou bless me.

And he said unto him, What is thy name? And he said, Jacob.

And he said, Thy name shall be called no more Jacob, but ISRAEL: for as a prince hast thou power with God and with men, and hast prevailed.

And Jacob asked him, and said, Tell me, I pray thee, thy name. And he said, Wherefore is it that thou dost ask after my name? And he blessed him there.

And Jacob called the name of the place Peniel: for I have seen God face to face, and my life is preserved.

Exodus 23:20 & 23-31:

Behold, I send an Angel before thee, to keep thee in the way, and to bring thee into the place which I have prepared.

For mine Angel shall go before thee, and bring thee in unto the Amorites, and the Hittites, and the Perizzites, and the Canaanites, and the Hivites, and the Jebusites: and I will cut them off.

Thou shalt not bow down to their gods, nor serve them, nor do after their works: but thou shalt utterly overthrow them, and quite break down their images.

And ye shall serve the Lord your God, and He shall bless thy bread, and thy water; and I will take sickness away from the midst of thee.

There shall nothing cast their young, nor be barren, in thy land: the number of thy days I will fulfil.

I will send my fear before thee, and will destroy all the people to whom thou shalt come, and I will make all thine enemies turn their backs unto thee.

And I will send hornets before thee, which shall drive out the Hivite, the Canaanite, and the Hittite, from before thee.

I will not drive them out from before thee in one year; lest the land become desolate, and the beast of the field multiply against thee.

By little and little I will drive them out from before thee, until thou be increased, and inherit the land.

And I will set thy bounds from the Red sea even unto the sea of the Philistines, and from the desert unto the river: for I will deliver the inhabitants of the land into your hand; and thou shalt drive them out before thee.

Deuteronomy 28:1-14:

And it shall come to pass, if thou shalt hearken diligently unto the voice of the Lord thy God, to observe and to do all his commandments which I command thee this day, that the Lord thy God will set thee on high above all nations of the earth:

And all these blessings shall come on thee, and overtake thee, if thou shalt hearken unto the voice of the Lord thy God.

Blessed shalt thou be in the city, and blessed shalt thou be in the field.

Blessed shall be the fruit of thy body, and the fruit of thy ground, and the fruit of thy cattle, the increase of thy kine, and the flocks of thy sheep.

Blessed shall be thy basket and thy store.

Blessed shalt thou be when thou comest in, and blessed shalt thou be when thou goest out.

The Lord shall cause thine enemies that rise up against thee to be smitten before thy face: they shall come out against thee one way, and flee before thee seven ways.

The Lord shall command the blessing upon thee in thy storehouses, and in all that thou settest thine hand unto; and he shall bless thee in the land which the Lord thy God giveth thee.

The Lord shall establish thee an holy people unto himself, as he hath sworn unto thee, if thou shalt keep the commandments of the Lord thy God, and walk in his ways.

And all people of the earth shall see that thou art called by the name of Lord; and they shall be afraid of thee.

And the Lord shall make thee plenteous in goods, in the fruit of thy body, and in the fruit of thy cattle, and in the fruit of thy ground, in the land which the Lord sware unto thy fathers to give thee.

The Lord shall open unto thee his good treasure, the heaven to give the rain unto thy land in his season, and to bless all the work of thine hand: and thou shalt lend unto many nations, and thou shalt not borrow.

And the Lord shall make thee the head, and not the tail; and thou shalt be above only, and thou shalt not be beneath; if that thou hearken unto the commandments of the Lord thy God, which I command thee this day, to observe and to do them:

And thou shalt not go aside from any of the words which I command thee this day, to the right hand, or to the left, to go after other gods to serve them.

Deuteronomy 30:1-10:

And it shall come to pass, when all these things are come upon thee, the blessing and the curse, which I have set before thee, and thou shalt call them to mind among all the nations, whither the Lord thy God hath driven thee,

And shalt return unto the Lord thy God, and shalt obey his voice according to all that I command thee this day, thou and thy children, with all thine heart, and with all thy soul;

That then the Lord thy God will turn thy captivity, and have compassion upon thee, and will return and gather thee from all the nations, whither the Lord thy God hath scattered thee.

If any of thine be driven out unto the outmost parts of

heaven, from thence will the Lord thy God gather thee, and from thence will he fetch thee:

And the Lord thy God will bring thee into the land which thy fathers possessed, and thou shalt possess it; and he will do thee good, and multiply thee above thy fathers.

And the Lord thy God will circumcise thine heart, and the heart of thy seed, to love the Lord thy God with all thine heart, and with all thy soul, that thou mayest live.

And the Lord thy God will put all these curses upon thine enemies, and on them that hate thee, which persecuted thee.

And thou shalt return and obey the voice of the Lord, and do all his commandments which I command thee this day.

And the Lord thy God will make thee plenteous in every work of thine hand, in the fruit of thy body, and in the fruit of thy cattle, and in the fruit of thy land, for good: for the Lord will again rejoice over thee for good, as he rejoiced over thy fathers:

If thou shalt hearken unto the voice of the Lord thy God, to keep his commandments and his statutes which are written in this book of the law, and if thou turn unto the Lord thy God with all thine heart, and with all thy soul.

2 Samuel 6:12-19:

And it was told king David, saying, The Lord hath blessed the house of Obededom, and all that pertaineth unto him, because of the ark of God. So David went and brought up the ark of God from the house of Obededom into the city of David with gladness.

And it was so, that when they that bare the ark of the Lord had gone six paces, he sacrificed oxen and fatlings.

And David danced before the Lord with all his might; and David was girded with a linen ephod.

So David and all the house of ISRAEL brought up the ark of the Lord with shouting, and with the sound of the trumpet.

And as the ark of the Lord came into the city of David, Michal Saul's daughter looked through a window, and saw king David leaping and dancing before the Lord; and she despised him in her heart.

And they brought in the ark of the Lord, and set it in his place, in the midst of the tabernacle that David had pitched for it: and David offered burnt offerings and peace offerings before the Lord.

And as soon as David had made an end of offering burnt offerings and peace offerings, he blessed the people in the name of the Lord of hosts.

And he dealt among all the people, even among the whole multitude of ISRAEL, as well to the women as men, to every one a cake of bread, and a good piece of flesh, and a flagon of wine. So all the people departed every one to his house.

2 Samuel 7:4-12:

And it came to pass that night, that the word of the Lord came unto Nathan, saying,

Go and tell my servant David, Thus saith the Lord, Shalt thou build me an house for me to dwell in?

Whereas I have not dwelt in any house since the time that I brought up the children of ISRAEL out of Egypt, even to this day, but have walked in a tent and in a tabernacle.

In all the places wherein I have walked with all the children of ISRAEL spake I a word with any of the tribes of ISRAEL, whom I commanded to feed my people ISRAEL, saying, Why build ye not me an house of cedar?

Now therefore so shalt thou say unto my servant David, Thus saith the Lord of hosts, I took thee from the sheepcote, from following the sheep, to be ruler over my people, over IS-RAEL:

And I was with thee whithersoever thou wentest, and have cut off all thine enemies out of thy sight, and have made thee a great name, like unto the name of the great men that are in the earth.

Moreover I will appoint a place for my people ISRAEL, and will plant them, that they may dwell in a place of their own, and move no more; neither shall the children of wickedness afflict them any more, as beforetime,

And as since the time that I commanded judges to be over my people ISRAEL, and have caused thee to rest from all thine enemies. Also the Lord telleth thee that he will make thee an house.

And when thy days be fulfilled, and thou shalt sleep with thy fathers, I will set up thy seed after thee, which shall proceed out of thy bowels, and I will establish his kingdom.

2 Samuel 24:16-25:

And when the angel stretched out his hand upon JERUSA-LEM to destroy it, the Lord repented him of the evil, and said to the angel that destroyed the people, It is enough: stay now thine hand. And the angel of the Lord was by the threshingplace of Araunah the Jebusite.

And David spake unto the Lord when he saw the angel

that smote the people, and said, Lo, I have sinned, and I have done wickedly: but these sheep, what have they done? let thine hand, I pray thee, be against me, and against my father's house.

And Gad came that day to David, and said unto him, Go up, rear an altar unto the Lord in the threshingfloor of Araunah the Jebusite.

And David, according to the saying of Gad, went up as the Lord commanded.

And Araunah looked, and saw the king and his servants coming on toward him: and Araunah went out, and bowed himself before the king on his face upon the ground.

And Araunah said, Wherefore is my lord the king come to his servant? And David said, To buy the threshingfloor of thee, to build an altar unto the Lord, that the plague may be stayed from the people.

And Araunah said unto David, Let my lord the king take and offer up what seemeth good unto him: behold, here be oxen for burnt sacrifice, and threshing instruments and other instruments of the oxen for wood.

All these things did Araunah, as a king, give unto the king. And Araunah said unto the king, The Lord thy God accept thee.

And the king said unto Araunah, Nay; but I will surely buy it of thee at a price: neither will I offer burnt offerings unto the Lord my God of that which doth cost me nothing. So David bought the threshingfloor and the oxen for fifty shekels of silver.

And David built there an altar unto the Lord, and offered

burnt offerings and peace offerings. So the Lord was intreated for the land, and the plague was stayed from ISRAEL.

1 Chronicles 22:1-19:

Then David said, This is the house of the Lord God, and this is the altar of the burnt offering for ISRAEL.

And David commanded to gather together the strangers that were in the land of ISRAEL; and he set masons to hew wrought stones to build the house of God.

And David prepared iron in abundance for the nails for the doors of the gates, and for the joinings; and brass in abundance without weight;

Also cedar trees in abundance: for the Zidonians and they of Tyre brought much cedar wood to David.

And David said, Solomon my son is young and tender, and the house that is to be builded for the Lord must be exceeding magnifical, of fame and of glory throughout all countries: I will therefore now make preparation for it. So David prepared abundantly before his death.

Then he called for Solomon his son, and charged him to build an house for the Lord God of ISRAEL.

And David said to Solomon, My son, as for me, it was in my mind to build an house unto the name of the Lord my God:

But the word of the Lord came to me, saying, Thou hast shed blood abundantly, and hast made great wars: thou shalt not build an house unto my name, because thou hast shed much blood upon the earth in my sight.

Behold, a son shall be born to thee, who shall be a man of rest; and I will give him rest from all his enemies round about:

for his name shall be Solomon, and I will give peace and quietness unto ISRAEL in his days.

He shall build an house for my name; and he shall be my son, and I will be his father; and I will establish the throne of his kingdom over ISRAEL for ever.

Now, my son, the Lord be with thee; and prosper thou, and build the house of the Lord thy God, as he hath said of thee.

Only the Lord give thee wisdom and understanding, and give thee charge concerning ISRAEL, that thou mayest keep the law of the Lord thy God.

Then shalt thou prosper, if thou takest heed to fulfil the statutes and judgments which the Lord charged Moses with concerning ISRAEL: be strong, and of good courage; dread not, nor be dismayed.

Now, behold, in my trouble I have prepared for the house of the Lord an hundred thousand talents of gold, and a thousand thousand talents of silver; and of brass and iron without weight; for it is in abundance: timber also and stone have I prepared; and thou mayest add thereto.

Moreover there are workmen with thee in abundance, hewers and workers of stone and timber, and all manner of cunning men for every manner of work.

Of the gold, the silver, and the brass, and the iron, there is no number. Arise therefore, and be doing, and the Lord be with thee.

David also commanded all the princes of ISRAEL to help Solomon his son, saying,

Is not the Lord your God with you? and hath he not given

you rest on every side? for he hath given the inhabitants of the land into mine hand; and the land is subdued before the Lord, and before his people.

Now set your heart and your soul to seek the Lord your God; arise therefore, and build ye the sanctuary of the Lord God, to bring the ark of the covenant of the Lord, and the holy vessels of God, into the house that is to be built to the name of the Lord.

1 Chronicles 28:14-18:

He gave of gold by weight for things of gold, for all instruments of all manner of service; silver also for all instruments of silver by weight, for all instruments of every kind of service:

Even the weight for the candlesticks of gold, and for their lamps of gold, by weight for every candlestick, and for the lamps thereof: and for the candlesticks of silver by weight, both for the candlestick, and also for the lamps thereof, according to the use of every candlestick.

And by weight he gave gold for the tables of shewbread, for every table; and likewise silver for the tables of silver:

Also pure gold for the fleshhooks, and the bowls, and the cups: and for the golden basons he gave gold by weight for every bason; and likewise silver by weight for every bason of silver:

And for the altar of incense refined gold by weight; and gold for the pattern of the chariot of the Cherubims, that spread out their wings, and covered the ark of the covenant of the Lord.

1 Chronicles 29:1-5:

Furthermore David the king said unto all the congregation, Solomon my son, whom alone God hath chosen, is yet young and tender, and the work is great: for the palace is not for man, but for the Lord God.

Now I have prepared with all my might for the house of my God the gold for things to be made of gold, and the silver for things of silver, and the brass for things of brass, the iron for things of iron, and wood for things of wood; onyx stones, and stones to be set, glistering stones, and of divers colours, and all manner of precious stones, and marble stones in abundance.

Moreover, because I have set my affection to the house of my God, I have of mine own proper good, of gold and silver, which I have given to the house of my God, over and above all that I have prepared for the holy house.

Even three thousand talents of gold, of the gold of Ophir, and seven thousand talents of refined silver, to overlay the walls of the houses withal:

The gold for things of gold, and the silver for things of silver, and for all manner of work to be made by the hands of artificers. And who then is willing to consecrate his service this day unto the Lord?

Nehemiah 2:1-6:

And it came to pass in the month Nisan, in the twentieth year of Artaxerxes the king, that wine was before him: and I took up the wine, and gave it unto the king. Now I had not been beforetime sad in his presence.

Wherefore the king said unto me, Why is thy countenance

sad, seeing thou art not sick? this is nothing else but sorrow of heart. Then I was very sore afraid,

And said unto the king, Let the king live for ever: why should not my countenance be sad, when the city, the place of my fathers' sepulchres, lieth waste, and the gates thereof are consumed with fire?

Then the king said unto me, For what dost thou make request? So I prayed to the God of heaven.

And I said unto the king, If it please the king, and if thy servant have found favour in thy sight, that thou wouldest send me unto Judah, unto the city of my fathers' sepulchres, that I may build it.

And the king said unto me, (the queen also sitting by him,) For how long shall thy journey be? and when wilt thou return? So it pleased the king to send me; and I set him a time.

Psalms 51:1-19:

Have mercy upon me, O God, according to thy loving-kindness: according unto the multitude of thy tender mercies blot out my transgressions.

Wash me throughly from mine iniquity, and cleanse me from my sin.

For I acknowledge my transgressions: and my sin is ever before me.

Against thee, thee only, have I sinned, and done this evil in thy sight: that thou mightest be justified when thou speakest, and be clear when thou judgest.

Behold, I was shapen in iniquity; and in sin did my mother conceive me.

Behold, thou desirest truth in the inward parts: and in the

hidden part thou shalt make me to know wisdom.

Purge me with hyssop, and I shall be clean: wash me, and I shall be whiter than snow.

Make me to hear joy and gladness; that the bones which thou hast broken may rejoice.

Hide thy face from my sins, and blot out all mine iniquities.

Create in me a clean heart, O God; and renew a right spirit within me.

Cast me not away from thy presence; and take not thy holy spirit from me.

Restore unto me the joy of thy salvation; and uphold me with thy free spirit.

Then will I teach transgressors thy ways; and sinners shall be converted unto thee.

Deliver me from bloodguiltiness, O God, thou God of my salvation: and my tongue shall sing aloud of thy righteousness.

O Lord, open thou my lips; and my mouth shall shew forth thy praise.

For thou desirest not sacrifice; else would I give it: thou delightest not in burnt offering.

The sacrifices of God are a broken spirit: a broken and a contrite heart, O God, thou wilt not despise.

Do good in thy good pleasure unto ZION: build thou the walls of JERUSALEM.

Then shalt thou be pleased with the sacrifices of righteousness, with burnt offering and whole burnt offering: then shall they offer bullocks upon thine altar.

Psalms 72:1-20:

Give the king thy judgments, O God, and thy righteousness unto the king's son.

He shall judge thy people with righteousness, and thy poor with judgment.

The mountains shall bring peace to the people, and the little hills, by righteousness.

He shall judge the poor of the people, he shall save the children of the needy, and shall break in pieces the oppressor.

They shall fear thee as long as the sun and moon endure, throughout all generations.

He shall come down like rain upon the mown grass: as showers that water the earth.

In his days shall the righteous flourish; and abundance of peace so long as the moon endureth.

He shall have dominion also from sea to sea, and from the river unto the ends of the earth.

They that dwell in the wilderness shall bow before him; and his enemies shall lick the dust.

The kings of Tarshish and of the isles shall bring presents: the kings of Sheba and Seba shall offer gifts.

Yea, all kings shall fall down before him: all nations shall serve him.

For he shall deliver the needy when he crieth; the poor also, and him that hath no helper.

He shall spare the poor and needy, and shall save the souls of the needy.

He shall redeem their soul from deceit and violence: and precious shall their blood be in his sight.

And he shall live, and to him shall be given of the gold of Sheba: prayer also shall be made for him continually; and daily shall he be praised.

There shall be an handful of corn in the earth upon the top of the mountains; the fruit thereof shall shake like Lebanon: and they of the city shall flourish like grass of the earth.

His name shall endure for ever: his name shall be continued as long as the sun: and men shall be blessed in him: all nations shall call him blessed.

Blessed be the Lord God, the God of ISRAEL, who only doeth wondrous things.

And blessed be his glorious name for ever: and let the whole earth be filled with his glory; Amen, and Amen.

The prayers of David the son of Jesse are ended.

Psalms 137:1-6:

By the rivers of Babylon, there we sat down, yea, we wept, when we remembered ZION.

We hanged our harps upon the willows in the midst thereof.

For there they that carried us away captive required of us a song; and they that wasted us required of us mirth, saying, Sing us one of the songs of ZION.

How shall we sing the Lord's song in a strange land?

If I forget thee, O JERUSALEM, let my right hand forget her cunning.

If I do not remember thee, let my tongue cleave to the roof of my mouth; if I prefer not JERUSALEM above my chief joy.

Isaiah 11:1-12:5:

And there shall come forth a rod out of the stem of Jesse, and a Branch shall grow out of his roots:

And the spirit of the Lord shall rest upon him, the spirit of wisdom and understanding, the spirit of counsel and might, the spirit of knowledge and of the fear of the Lord;

And shall make him of quick understanding in the fear of the Lord: and he shall not judge after the sight of his eyes, neither reprove after the hearing of his ears:

But with righteousness shall he judge the poor, and reprove with equity for the meek of the earth: and he shall smite the earth: with the rod of his mouth, and with the breath of his lips shall he slay the wicked.

And righteousness shall be the girdle of his loins, and faithfulness the girdle of his reins.

The wolf also shall dwell with the lamb, and the leopard shall lie down with the kid; and the calf and the young lion and the fatling together; and a little child shall leadthem.

And the cow and the bear shall feed; their young ones shall lie down together: and the lion shall eat straw like the ox.

And the sucking child shall play on the hole of the asp, and the weaned child shall put his hand on the cockatrice' den.

They shall not hurt nor destroy in all my holy mountain: for the earth shall be full of the knowledge of the Lord, as the waters cover the sea.

And in that day there shall be a root of Jesse, which shall stand for an ensign of the people; to it shall the Gentiles seek: and his rest shall be glorious.

And it shall come to pass in that day, that the Lord shall set his hand again the second time to recover the remnant of his people, which shall be left, from Assyria, and from Egypt, and from Pathros, and from Cush, and from Elam, and from Shinar, and from Hamath, and from the islands of the sea.

And he shall set up an ensign for the nations, and shall assemble the outcasts of ISRAEL, and gather together the dispersed of Judah from the four corners of the earth.

The envy also of Ephraim shall depart, and the adversaries of Judah shall be cut off: Ephraim shall not envy Judah, and Judah shall not vex Ephraim.

But they shall fly upon the shoulders of the Philistines toward the west; they shall spoil them of the east together: they shall lay their hand upon Edom and Moab; and the children of Ammon shall obey them.

And the Lord shall utterly destroy the tongue of the Egyptian sea; and with his mighty wind shall he shake his hand over the river, and shall smite it in the seven streams, and make men go over dryshod.

And there shall be an highway for the remnant of his people, which shall be left, from Assyria; like as it was to ISRAEL in the day that he came up out of the land of Egypt.

And in that day thou shalt say, O Lord, I will praise thee: though thou wast angry with me, thine anger is turned away, and thou comfortedst me.

Behold, God is my salvation; I will trust, and not be afraid: for the Lord Jehovah is my strength and my song; he also is become my salvation.

Therefore with joy shall ye draw water out of the wells of salvation.

And in that day shall ye say, Praise the Lord, call upon his name, declare his doings among the people, make mention that his name is exalted.

Sing unto the Lord; for he hath done excellent things: this is known in all the earth.

Isaiah 19:23-25:

In that day shall there be a highway out of Egypt to Assyria, and the Assyrian shall come into Egypt, and the Egyptian into Assyria, and the Egyptians shall serve with the Assyrians.

In that day shall ISRAEL be the third with Egypt and with Assyria, even a blessing in the midst of the land:

Whom the Lord of hosts shall bless, saying, Blessed be Egypt my people, and Assyria the work of my hands, and IS-RAEL mine inheritance.

Isaiah 26:12-19:

Lord, thou wilt ordain peace for us: for thou also hast wrought all our works in us.

O Lord our God, other lords beside thee have had dominion over us: but by thee only will we make mention of thy name.

They are dead, they shall not live; they are deceased, they shall not rise: therefore hast thou visited and destroyed them, and made all their memory to perish.

Thou hast increased the nation, O Lord, thou hast increased the nation: thou art glorified: thou hadst removed it far unto all the ends of the earth.

Lord, in trouble have they visited thee, they poured out a prayer when thy chastening was upon them.

Like as a woman with child, that draweth near the time of her delivery, is in pain, and crieth out in her pangs; so have we been in thy sight, O Lord.

We have been with child, we have been in pain, we have as it were brought forth wind; we have not wrought any deliverance in the earth; neither have the inhabitants of the world fallen.

Thy dead men shall live, together with my dead body shall they arise. Awake and sing, ye that dwell in dust: for thy dew is as the dew of herbs, and the earth shall cast out the dead.

Isaiah 51:1-23:

Hearken to me, ye that follow after righteousness, ye that seek the Lord: look unto the rock whence ye are hewn, and to the hole of the pit whence ye are digged.

Look unto Abraham your father, and unto Sarah that bare you: for I called him alone, and blessed him, and increased him.

For the Lord shall comfort ZION: he will comfort all her waste places; and he will make her wilderness like Eden, and her desert like the garden of the Lord; joy and gladness shall be found therein, thanksgiving, and the voice of melody.

Hearken unto me, my people; and give ear unto me, O my nation: for a law shall proceed from me, and I will make my judgment to rest for a light of the people.

My righteousness is near; my salvation is gone forth, and

mine arms shall judge the people; the isles shall wait upon me, and on mine arm shall they trust.

Lift up your eyes to the heavens, and look upon the earth beneath: for the heavens shall vanish away like smoke, and the earth shall wax old like a garment, and they that dwell therein shall die in like manner: but my salvation shall be for ever, and my righteousness shall not be abolished.

Hearken unto me, ye that know righteousness, the people in whose heart is my law; fear ye not the reproach of men, neither be ye afraid of their revilings.

For the moth shall eat them up like a garment, and the worm shall eat them like wool: but my righteousness shall be for ever, and my salvation from generation to generation.

Awake, awake, put on strength, O arm of the Lord; awake, as in the ancient days, in the generations of old. Art thou not it that hath cut Rahab, and wounded the dragon?

Art thou not it which hath dried the sea, the waters of the great deep; that hath made the depths of the sea a way for the ransomed to pass over?

Therefore the redeemed of the Lord shall return, and come with singing unto ZION; and everlasting joy shall be upon their head: they shall obtain gladness and joy; and sorrow and mourning shall flee away.

I, even I, am he that comforteth you: who art thou, that thou shouldest be afraid of a man that shall die, and of the son of man which shall be made as grass;

And forgettest the Lord thy maker, that hath stretched forth the heavens, and laid the foundations of the earth; and hast feared continually every day because of the fury of the oppressor, as if he were ready to destroy? and where is the fury of the oppressor?

The captive exile hasteneth that he may be loosed, and that he should not die in the pit, nor that his bread should fail.

But I am the Lord thy God, that divided the sea, whose waves roared: The Lord of hosts is his name.

And I have put my words in thy mouth, and I have covered thee in the shadow of mine hand, that I may plant the heavens, and lay the foundations of the earth, and say unto ZION, Thou art my people.

Awake, awake, stand up, O JERUSALEM, which hast drunk at the hand of the Lord the cup of his fury; thou hast drunken the dregs of the cup of trembling, and wrung them out.

There is none to guide her among all the sons whom she hath brought forth; neither is there any that taketh her by the hand of all the sons that she hath brought up.

These two things are come unto thee; who shall be sorry for thee? desolation, and destruction, and the famine, and the sword: by whom shall I comfort thee?

Thy sons have fainted, they lie at the head of all the streets, as a wild bull in a net: they are full of the fury of the Lord, the rebuke of thy God.

Therefore hear now this, thou afflicted, and drunken, but not with wine:

Thus saith thy Lord the Lord, and thy God that pleadeth the cause of his people, Behold, I have taken out of thine hand the cup of trembling, even the dregs of the cup of my fury; thou shalt no more drink it again:

But I will put it into the hand of them that afflict thee; which have said to thy soul, Bow down, that we may go over: and thou hast laid thy body as the ground, and as the street, to them that went over.

Isaiah 60:1-22:

Arise, shine; for thy light is come, and the glory of the Lord is risen upon thee.

For, behold, the darkness shall cover the earth, and gross darkness the people: but the Lord shall arise upon thee, and his glory shall be seen upon thee.

And the Gentiles shall come to thy light, and kings to the brightness of thy rising.

Lift up thine eyes round about, and see: all they gather themselves together, they come to thee: thy sons shall come from far, and thy daughters shall be nursed at thy side.

Then thou shalt see, and flow together, and thine heart shall fear, and be enlarged; because the abundance of the sea shall be converted unto thee, the forces of the Gentiles shall come unto thee.

The multitude of camels shall cover thee, the dromedaries of Midian and Ephah; all they from Sheba shall come: they shall bring gold and incense; and they shall shew forth the praises of the Lord.

All the flocks of Kedar shall be gathered together unto thee, the rams of Nebaioth shall minister unto thee: they shall come up with acceptance on mine altar, and I will glorify the house of my glory.

Who are these that fly as a cloud, and as the doves to their windows?

Surely the isles shall wait for me, and the ships of Tarshish first, to bring thy sons from far, their silver and their gold with them, unto the name of the Lord thy God, and to the Holy One of ISRAEL, because he hath glorified thee.

And the sons of strangers shall build up thy walls, and their kings shall minister unto thee: for in my wrath I smote thee, but in my favour have I had mercy on thee.

Therefore thy gates shall be open continually; they shall not be shut day nor night; that men may bring unto thee the forces of the Gentiles, and that their kings may be brought.

For the nation and kingdom that will not serve thee shall perish; yea, those nations shall be utterly wasted.

The glory of Lebanon shall come unto thee, the fir tree, the pine tree, and the box together, to beautify the place of my sanctuary; and I will make the place of my feet glorious.

The sons also of them that afflicted thee shall come bending unto thee; and all they that despised thee shall bow themselves down at the soles of thy feet; and they shall call thee; The city of the Lord, The ZION of the Holy One of ISRAEL.

Whereas thou hast been forsaken and hated, so that no man went through thee, I will make thee an eternal excellency, a joy of many generations.

Thou shalt also suck the milk of the Gentiles, and shalt suck the breast of kings: and thou shalt know that I the Lord am thy Saviour and thy Redeemer, the mighty One of Jacob.

For brass I will bring gold, and for iron I will bring silver, and for wood brass, and for stones iron: I will also make thy officers peace, and thine exactors righteousness.

Violence shall no more be heard in thy land, wasting nor

destruction within thy borders; but thou shalt call thy walls Salvation, and thy gates Praise.

The sun shall be no more thy light by day; neither for brightness shall the moon give light unto thee: but the Lord shall be unto thee an everlasting light, and thy God thy glory.

Thy sun shall no more go down; neither shall thy moon withdraw itself: for the Lord shall be thine everlasting light, and the days of thy mourning shall be ended.

Thy people also shall be all righteous: they shall inherit the land for ever, the branch of my planting, the work of my hands, that I may be glorified.

A little one shall become a thousand, and a small one a strong nation: I the Lord will hasten it in his time.

Isaiah 61:4-9:
And they shall build the old wastes, they shall raise up the former desolations, and they shall repair the waste cities, the desolations of many generations.

And strangers shall stand and feed your flocks, and the sons of the alien shall be your plowmen and your vinedressers.

But ye shall be named the Priests of the Lord: men shall call you the Ministers of our God: ye shall eat the riches of the Gentiles, and in their glory shall ye boast yourselves.

For your shame ye shall have double; and for confusion they shall rejoice in their portion: therefore in their land they shall possess the double: everlasting joy shall be unto them.

For I the Lord love judgment, I hate robbery for burnt offering; and I will direct their work in truth, and I will make an everlasting covenant with them.

And their seed shall be known among the Gentiles, and

their offspring among the people: all that see them shall acknowledge them, that they are the seed which the Lord hath blessed.

Isaiah 62:1-12:

For ZION's sake will I not hold my peace, and for JERUSALEM's sake I will not rest, until the righteousness thereof go forth as brightness, and the salvation thereof as a lamp that burneth.

And the Gentiles shall see thy righteousness, and all kings thy glory: and thou shalt be called by a new name, which the mouth of the Lord shall name.

Thou shalt also be a crown of glory in the hand of the Lord, and a royal diadem in the hand of thy God.

Thou shalt no more be termed Forsaken; neither shall thy land any more be termed Desolate: but thou shalt be called Hephzibah, and thy land Beulah: for the Lord delighteth in thee, and thy land shall be married.

For as a young man marrieth a virgin, so shall thy sons marry thee: and as the bridegroom rejoiceth over the bride, so shall thy God rejoice over thee.

I have set watchmen upon thy walls, O JERUSALEM, which shall never hold their peace day nor night: ye that make mention of the Lord, keep not silence,

And give him no rest, till he establish, and till he make JERUSALEM a praise in the earth.

The Lord hath sworn by his right hand, and by the arm of his strength, Surely I will no more give thy corn to be meat for thine enemies; and the sons of the stranger shall not drink thy wine, for the which thou hast laboured:

But they that have gathered it shall eat it, and praise the Lord; and they that have brought it together shall drink it in the courts of my holiness.

Go through, go through the gates; prepare ye the way of the people; cast up, cast up the highway; gather out the stones; lift up a standard for the people.

Behold, the Lord hath proclaimed unto the end of the world, Say ye to the daughter of ZION, Behold, thy salvation cometh; behold, his reward is with him, and his work before him.

And they shall call them, The holy people, The redeemed of the Lord: and thou shalt be called, Sought out, A city not forsaken.

Isaiah 66:5-22:

Hear the word of the Lord, ye that tremble at his word; Your brethren that hated you, that cast you out for my name's sake, said, Let the Lord be glorified: but he shall appear to your joy, and they shall be ashamed.

A voice of noise from the city, a voice from the temple, a voice of the Lord that rendereth recompence to his enemies.

Before she travailed, she brought forth; before her pain came, she was delivered of a man child.

Who hath heard such a thing? who hath seen such things? Shall the earth be made to bring forth in one day? or shall a nation be born at once? for as soon as ZION travailed, she brought forth her children.

Shall I bring to the birth, and not cause to bring forth? saith the Lord: shall I cause to bring forth, and shut the womb? saith thy God.

Rejoice ye with JERUSALEM, and be glad with her, all ye that love her: rejoice for joy with her, all ye that mourn for her:

That ye may suck, and be satisfied with the breasts of her consolations; that ye may milk out, and be delighted with the abundance of her glory.

For thus saith the Lord, Behold, I will extend peace to her like a river, and the glory of the Gentiles like a flowing stream: then shall ye suck, ye shall be borne upon her sides, and be dandled upon her knees.

As one whom his mother comforteth, so will I comfort you; and ye shall be comforted in JERUSALEM.

And when ye see this, your heart shall rejoice, and your bones shall flourish like an herb: and the hand of the Lord shall be known toward his servants, and his indignation toward his enemies.

For, behold, the Lord will come with fire, and with his chariots like a whirlwind, to render his anger with fury, and his rebuke with flames of fire.

For by fire and by his sword will the Lord plead with all flesh: and the slain of the Lord shall be many.

They that sanctify themselves, and purify themselves in the gardens behind one tree in the midst, eating swine's flesh, and the abomination, and the mouse, shall be consumed together, saith the Lord.

For I know their works and their thoughts: it shall come, that I will gather all nations and tongues; and they shall come, and see my glory.

And I will set a sign among them, and I will send those that escape of them unto the nations, to Tarshish, Pul, and Lud, that draw the bow, to Tubal, and Javan, to the isles afar off, that have not heard my fame, neither have seen my glory; and they shall declare my glory among the Gentiles.

And they shall bring all your brethren for an offering unto the Lord out of all nations upon horses, and in chariots, and in litters, and upon mules, and upon swift beasts, to my holy mountain JERUSALEM, saith the Lord, as the children of ISRAEL bring an offering in a clean vessel into the house of the Lord.

And I will also take of them for priests and for Levites, saith the Lord.

For as the new heavens and the new earth, which I will make, shall remain before me, saith the Lord, so shall your seed and your name remain.

Jeremiah 3:14-18:

Turn, O backsliding children, saith the Lord; for I am married unto you: and I will take you one of a city, and two of a family, and I will bring you to ZION:

And I will give you pastors according to mine heart, which shall feed you with knowledge and understanding.

And it shall come to pass, when ye be multiplied and increased in the land, in those days, saith the Lord, they shall say no more, The ark of the covenant of the Lord: neither shall it come to mind: neither shall they remember it; neither shall they visit it; neither shall that be done any more.

At that time they shall call JERUSALEM the throne of the Lord; and all the nations shall be gathered unto it, to the name of the Lord, to JERUSALEM: neither shall they walk any more after the imagination of their evil heart.

In those days the house of Judah shall walk with the house of ISRAEL, and they shall come together out of the land of the north to the land that I have given for an inheritance unto your fathers.

Jeremiah 4:3-18:

For thus saith the Lord to the men of Judah and JERUSA-LEM, Break up your fallow ground, and sow not among thorns.

Circumcise yourselves to the Lord, and take away the fore-skins of your heart, ye men of Judah and inhabitants of JERUSALEM: lest my fury come forth like fire, and burn that none can quench it, because of the evil of your doings.

Declare ye in Judah, and publish in JERUSALEM; and say, Blow ye the trumpet in the land: cry, gather together, and say, Assemble yourselves, and let us go into the defenced cities.

Set up the standard toward ZION: retire, stay not: for I will bring evil from the north, and a great destruction.

The lion is come up from his thicket, and the destroyer of the Gentiles is on his way; he is gone forth from his place to make thy land desolate; and thy cities shall be laid waste, without an inhabitant.

For this gird you with sackcloth, lament and howl: for the fierce anger of the Lord is not turned back from us.

And it shall come to pass at that day, saith the Lord, that the heart of the king shall perish, and the heart of the princes; and the priests shall be astonished, and the prophets shall wonder.

Then said I, Ah, Lord God! surely thou hast greatly deceived this people and JERUSALEM, saying, Ye shall have peace; whereas the sword reacheth unto the soul.

At that time shall it be said to this people and to JERUSA-LEM, A dry wind of the high places in the wilderness toward the daughter of my people, not to fan, nor to cleanse,

Even a full wind from those places shall come unto me: now also will I give sentence against them.

Behold, he shall come up as clouds, and his chariots shall be as a whirlwind: his horses are swifter than eagles. Woe unto us! for we are spoiled.

O JERUSALEM, wash thine heart from wickedness, that thou mayest be saved. How long shall thy vain thoughts lodge within thee?

For a voice declareth from Dan, and publisheth affliction from mount Ephraim.

Make ye mention to the nations; behold, publish against JERUSALEM, that watchers come from a far country, and give out their voice against the cities of Judah.

As keepers of a field, are they against her round about; because she hath been rebellious against me, saith the Lord.

Thy way and thy doings have procured these things unto thee; this is thy wickedness, because it is bitter, because it reacheth unto thine heart.

Jeremiah 24:1-7:
The Lord shewed me, and, behold, two baskets of figs were set before the temple of the Lord, after that Nebuchadrezzar king of Babylon had carried away captive Jeconiah the son of Jehoiakim king of Judah, and the princes of Judah, with the carpenters and smiths, from JERUSALEM, and had brought them to Babylon.

One basket had very good figs, even like the figs that are first ripe: and the other basket had very naughty figs, which could not be eaten, they were so bad.

Then said the Lord unto me, What seest thou, Jeremiah? And I said, Figs; the good figs, very good; and the evil, very evil, that cannot be eaten, they are so evil.

Again the word of the Lord came unto me, saying,

Thus saith the Lord, the God of ISRAEL; Like these good figs, so will I acknowledge them that are carried away captive of Judah, whom I have sent out of this place into the land of the Chaldeans for their good.

For I will set mine eyes upon them for good, and I will bring them again to this land: and I will build them, and not pull them down; and I will plant them, and not pluck them up.

And I will give them an heart to know me, that I am the Lord: and they shall be my people, and I will be their God: for they shall return unto me with their whole heart.

Jeremiah 30:3-22:

For, lo, the days come, saith the Lord, that I will bring again the captivity of my people ISRAEL and Judah, saith the Lord: and I will cause them to return to the land that I gave to their fathers, and they shall possess it.

And these are the words that the Lord spake concerning ISRAEL and concerning Judah.

For thus saith the Lord; We have heard a voice of trembling, of fear, and not of peace.

Ask ye now, and see whether a man doth travail with child? wherefore do I see every man with his hands on his loins, as a woman in travail, and all faces are turned into paleness?

Alas! for that day is great, so that none is like it: it is even the time of Jacob's trouble, but he shall be saved out of it.

For it shall come to pass in that day, saith the Lord of hosts, that I will break his yoke from off thy neck, and will burst thy bonds, and strangers shall no more serve themselves of him:

But they shall serve the Lord their God, and David their king, whom I will raise up unto them.

Therefore fear thou not, O my servant Jacob, saith the Lord; neither be dismayed, O ISRAEL: for, lo, I will save thee from afar, and thy seed from the land of their captivity; and Jacob shall return, and shall be in rest, and be quiet, and none shall make him afraid.

For I am with thee, saith the Lord, to save thee: though I make a full end of all nations whither I have scattered thee, yet will I not make a fu tll end of thee: but I will correct thee in measure, and will not leave thee altogether unpunished.

For thus saith the Lord, Thy bruise is incurable, and thy wound is grievous.

There is none to plead thy cause, that thou mayest be bound up: thou hast no healing medicines.

All thy lovers have forgotten thee; they seek thee not; for I have wounded thee with the wound of an enemy, with the chastisement of a cruel one, for the multitude of thine iniquity; because thy sins were increased.

Why criest thou for thine affliction? thy sorrow is incurable for the multitude of thine iniquity: because thy sins were increased, I have done these things unto thee.

Therefore all they that devour thee shall be devoured; and all thine adversaries, every one of them, shall go into captivity;

and they that spoil thee shall be a spoil, and all that prey upon thee will I give for a prey.

For I will restore health unto thee, and I will heal thee of thy wounds, saith the Lord; because they called thee an Outcast, saying, This is ZION, whom no man seeketh after.

Thus saith the Lord; Behold, I will bring again the captivity of Jacob's tents, and have mercy on his dwellingplaces; and the city shall be builded upon her own heap, and the palace shall remain after the manner thereof.

And out of them shall proceed thanksgiving and the voice of them that make merry: and I will multiply them, and they shall not be few; I will also glorify them, and they shall not be small.

Their children also shall be as aforetime, and their congregation shall be established before me, and I will punish all that oppress them.

And their nobles shall be of themselves, and their governor shall proceed from the midst of them; and I will cause him to draw near, and he shall approach unto me: for who is this that engaged his heart to approach unto me? saith the Lord.

And ye shall be my people, and I will be your God.

Jeremiah 32:36-44:

And now therefore thus saith the Lord, the God of ISRAEL, concerning this city, whereof ye say, It shall be delivered into the hand of the king of Babylon by the sword, and by the famine, and by the pestilence;

Behold, I will gather them out of all countries, whither I have driven them in mine anger, and in my fury, and in great wrath; and I will bring them again unto this place, and I will cause them to dwell safely:

And they shall be my people, and I will be their God:

And I will give them one heart, and one way, that they may fear me for ever, for the good of them, and of their children after them:

And I will make an everlasting covenant with them, that I will not turn away from them, to do them good; but I will put my fear in their hearts, that they shall not depart from me.

Yea, I will rejoice over them to do them good, and I will plant them in this land assuredly with my whole heart and with my whole soul.

For thus saith the Lord; Like as I have brought all this great evil upon this people, so will I bring upon them all the good that I have promised them.

And fields shall be bought in this land, whereof ye say, It is desolate without man or beast; it is given into the hand of the Chaldeans.

Men shall buy fields for money, and subscribe evidences, and seal them, and take witnesses in the land of Benjamin, and in the places about JERUSALEM, and in the cities of Judah, and in the cities of the mountains, and in the cities of the valley, and in the cities of the south: for I will cause their captivity to return, saith the Lord.

Jeremiah 33:1-26:

Moreover the word of the Lord came unto Jeremiah the second time, while he was yet shut up in the court of the prison, saying,

Thus saith the Lord the maker thereof, the Lord that formed it, to establish it; the Lord is his name;

Call unto me, and I will answer thee, and shew thee great and mighty things, which thou knowest not.

For thus saith the Lord, the God of ISRAEL, concerning the houses of this city, and concerning the houses of the kings of Judah, which are thrown down by the mounts, and by the sword;

They come to fight with the Chaldeans, but it is to fill them with the dead bodies of men, whom I have slain in mine anger and in my fury, and for all whose wickedness I have hid my face from this city.

Behold, I will bring it health and cure, and I will cure them and will reveal unto them the abundance of peace and truth.

And I will cause the captivity of Judah and the captivity of ISRAEL to return, and will build them, as at the first.

And I will cleanse them from all their iniquity, whereby they have sinned against me; and I will pardon all their iniquities, whereby they have sinned, and whereby they have transgressed against me.

And it shall be to me a name of joy, a praise and an honour before all the nations of the earth, which shall hear all the good that I do unto them: and they shall fear and tremble for all the goodness and for all the prosperity that I procure unto it.

Thus saith the Lord; Again there shall be heard in this place, which ye say shall be desolate without man and without beast, even in the cities of Judah, and in the streets of JERUSALEM, that are desolate, without man, and without inhabitant, and without beast,

The voice of joy, and the voice of gladness, the voice of the bridegroom, and the voice of the bride, the voice of them that shall say, Praise the Lord of hosts: for the Lord is good; for his mercy endureth for ever: and of them that shall bring the sacrifice of praise into the house of the Lord. For I will cause to return the captivity of the land, as at the first, saith the Lord.

Thus saith the Lord of hosts; Again in this place, which is desolate without man and without beast, and in all the cities thereof, shall be an habitation of shepherds causing their flocks to lie down.

In the cities of the mountains, in the cities of the vale, and in the cities of the south, and in the land of Benjamin, and in the places about JERUSALEM, and in the cities of Judah, shall the flocks pass again under the hands of him that telleth them, saith the Lord.

Behold, the days come, saith the Lord, that I will perform that good thing which I have promised unto the house of IS-RAEL and to the house of Judah.

In those days, and at that time, will I cause the Branch of righteousness to grow up unto David; and he shall execute judgment and righteousness in the land.

In those days shall Judah be saved, and JERUSALEM shall dwell safely: and this is the name wherewith she shall be called, The Lord our righteousness.

For thus saith the Lord; David shall never want a man to sit upon the throne of the house of ISRAEL;

Neither shall the priests the Levites want a man before me to offer burnt offerings, and to kindle meat offerings, and to do sacrifice continually.

And the word of the Lord came unto Jeremiah, saying,

Thus saith the Lord; If ye can break my covenant of the day, and my covenant of the night, and that there should not be day and night in their season;

Then may also my covenant be broken with David my servant, that he should not have a son to reign upon his throne; and with the Levites the priests, my ministers.

As the host of heaven cannot be numbered, neither the sand of the sea measured: so will I multiply the seed of David my servant, and the Levites that minister unto me.

Moreover the word of the Lord came to Jeremiah, saying,

Considerest thou not what this people have spoken, saying, The two families which the Lord hath chosen, he hath even cast them off? thus they have despised my people, that they should be no more a nation before them.

Thus saith the Lord; If my covenant be not with day and night, and if I have not appointed the ordinances of heaven and earth;

Then will I cast away the seed of Jacob and David my servant, so that I will not take any of his seed to be rulers over the seed of Abraham, Isaac, and Jacob: for I will cause their captivity to return, and have mercy on them.

Ezekiel 37:1-28:

The hand of the Lord was upon me, and carried me out in the spirit of the Lord, and set me down in the midst of the valley which was full of bones,

And caused me to pass by them round about: and, behold,

there were very many in the open valley; and, lo, they were very dry.

And he said unto me, Son of man, can these bones live? and I answered, O Lord God, thou knowest.

Again he said unto me, Prophesy upon these bones, and say unto them, O ye dry bones, hear the word of the Lord.

Thus saith the Lord God unto these bones; Behold, I will cause breath to enter into you, and ye shall live:

And I will lay sinews upon you, and will bring up flesh upon you, and cover you with skin, and put breath in you, and ye shall live; and ye shall know that I am the Lord.

So I prophesied as I was commanded: and as I prophesied, there was a noise, and behold a shaking, and the bones came together, bone to his bone.

And when I beheld, lo, the sinews and the flesh came up upon them, and the skin covered them above: but there was no breath in them.

Then said he unto me, Prophesy unto the wind, prophesy, son of man, and say to the wind, Thus saith the Lord God; Come from the four winds, O breath, and breathe upon these slain, that they may live.

So I prophesied as he commanded me, and the breath came into them, and they lived, and stood up upon their feet, an exceeding great army.

Then he said unto me, Son of man, these bones are the whole house of ISRAEL: behold, they say, Our bones are dried, and our hope is lost: we are cut off for our parts.

Therefore prophesy and say unto them, Thus saith the Lord God; Behold, O my people, I will open your graves, and cause you to come up out of your graves, and bring you into the land of ISRAEL.

And ye shall know that I am the Lord, when I have opened your graves, O My people, and brought you up out of your graves,

And shall put my spirit in you, and ye shall live, and I shall place you in your own land: then shall ye know that I the Lord have spoken it, and performed it, saith the Lord.

The word of the Lord came again unto me, saying,

Moreover, thou son of man, take thee one stick, and write upon it, For Judah, and for the children of ISRAEL his companions: then take another stick, and write upon it, For Joseph, the stick of Ephraim and for all the house of ISRAEL his companions:

And join them one to another into one stick; and they shall become one in thine hand.

And when the children of thy people shall speak unto thee, saying, Wilt thou not shew us what thou meanest by these?

Say unto them, Thus saith the Lord God; Behold, I will take the stick of Joseph, which is in the hand of Ephraim, and the tribes of ISRAEL his fellows, and will put them with him, even with the stick of Judah, and make them one stick, and they shall be one in mine hand.

And the sticks whereon thou writest shall be in thine hand before their eyes.

And say unto them, Thus saith the Lord God; Behold, I will take the children of ISRAEL from among the heathen, whither they be gone, and will gather them on every side, and bring them into their own land:

And I will make them one nation in the land upon the mountains of ISRAEL; and one king shall be king to them all: and they shall be no more two nations, neither shall they be divided into two kingdoms any more at all.

Neither shall they defile themselves any more with their idols, nor with their detestable things, nor with any of their transgressions: but I will save them out of all their dwellingplaces, wherein they have sinned, and will cleanse them: so shall they be my people, and I will be their God.

And David my servant shall be king over them; and they all shall have one shepherd: they shall also walk in my judgments, and observe my statutes, and do them.

And they shall dwell in the land that I have given unto Jacob my servant, wherein your fathers have dwelt; and they shall dwell therein, even they, and their children, and their children's children for ever: and my servant David shall be their prince for ever.

Moreover I will make a covenant of peace with them; it shall be an everlasting covenant with them: and I will place them, and multiply them, and will set my sanctuary in the midst of them for evermore.

My tabernacle also shall be with them: yea, I will be their God, and they shall be my people.

And the heathen shall know that I the Lord do sanctify ISRAEL, when my sanctuary shall be in the midst of them for evermore.

Hosea 2:14-23:

Therefore, behold, I will allure her, and bring her into the wilderness, and speak comfortably unto her.

And I will give her her vineyards from thence, and the valley of Achor for a door of hope: and she shall sing there, as in the days of her youth, and as in the day when she came up out of the land of Egypt.

And it shall be at that day, saith the Lord, that thou shalt call me Ishi; and shalt call me no more Baali.

For I will take away the names of Baalim out of her mouth, and they shall no more be remembered by their name.

And in that day will I make a covenant for them with the beasts of the field and with the fowls of heaven, and with the creeping things of the ground: and I will break the bow and the sword and the battle out of the earth, and will make them to lie down safely.

And I will betroth thee unto me for ever; yea, I will betroth thee unto me in righteousness, and in judgment, and in lovingkindness, and in mercies.

I will even betroth thee unto me in faithfulness: and thou shalt know the Lord.

And it shall come to pass in that day, I will hear, saith the Lord, I will hear the heavens, and they shall hear the earth;

And the earth shall hear the corn, and the wine, and the oil; and they shall hear Jezreel.

And I will sow her unto me in the earth; and I will have mercy upon her that had not obtained mercy; and I will say to them which were not my people, Thou art my people; and they shall say, Thou art my God.

Zechariah 1:14-21:

So the angel that communed with me said unto me, Cry

thou, saying, Thus saith the Lord of hosts; I am jealous for JERUSALEM and for ZION with a great jealousy.

And I am very sore displeased with the heathen that are at ease: for I was but a little displeased, and they helped forward the affliction.

Therefore thus saith the Lord; I am returned to JERUSA-LEM with mercies: my house shall be built in it, saith the Lord of hosts, and a line shall be stretched forth upon JERUSALEM.

Cry yet, saying, Thus saith the Lord of hosts; My cities through prosperity shall yet be spread abroad; and the Lord shall yet comfort ZION, and shall yet choose JERUSALEM.

Then lifted I up mine eyes, and saw, and behold four horns.

And I said unto the angel that talked with me, What be these? And he answered me, these are the horns which have scattered Judah, ISRAEL, and JERUSALEM.

And the Lord shewed me four carpenters.

Then said I, What come these to do? And he spake, saying, These are the horns which have scattered Judah, so that no man did lift up his head: but These are come to fray them, to cast out the horns of the Gentiles, which lifted up their horn over the land of Judah to scatter it.

Zechariah 8:1-23:

Again the word of the Lord of hosts came to me, saying,

Thus saith the Lord of hosts; I was jealous for ZION with great jealousy, and I was jealous for her with great fury.

Thus saith the Lord; I am returned unto ZION, and will dwell in the midst of JERUSALEM: and JERUSALEM shall be called a city of truth; and the mountain of the Lord of hosts the holy mountain.

Thus saith the Lord of hosts; There shall yet old men and old women dwell in the streets of JERUSALEM, and every man with his staff in his hand for very age.

And the streets of the city shall be full of boys and girls playing in the streets thereof.

Thus saith the Lord of hosts; If it be marvellous in the eyes of the remnant of this people in these days, should it also be marvellous in mine eyes? saith the Lord of hosts.

Thus saith the Lord of hosts; Behold, I will save my people from the east country, and from the west country;

And I will bring them, and they shall dwell in the midst of JERUSALEM: and they shall be my people, and I will be their God, in truth and in righteousness.

Thus saith the Lord of hosts; Let your hands be strong, ye that hear in these days these words by the mouth of the prophets, which were in the day that the foundation of the house of the Lord of hosts was laid, that the temple might be built.

For before these days there was no hire for man, nor any hire for beast; neither was there any peace to him that went out or came in because of the affliction: for I set all men every one against his neighbour.

But now I will not be unto the residue of this people as in the former days, saith the Lord of hosts.

For the seed shall be prosperous; the vine shall give her fruit, and the ground shall give her increase, and the heavens shall give their dew; and I will cause the remnant of this people to possess all these things.

And it shall come to pass, that as ye were a curse among the heathen, O house of Judah, and house of ISRAEL; so will I save you, and ye shall be a blessing: fear not, but let your hands be strong.

For thus saith the Lord of hosts; As I thought to punish you, when your fathers provoked me to wrath, saith the Lord of hosts, and I repented not:

So again have I thought in these days to do well unto JERU-SALEM and to the house of Judah: fear ye not.

These are the things that ye shall do; speak ye every man the truth to his neighbour; execute the judgment of truth and peace in your gates:

And let none of you imagine evil in your hearts against his neighbour; and love no false oath: for all these are things that I hate, saith the Lord.

And the word of the Lord of hosts came unto me, saying,

Thus saith the Lord of hosts; The fast of the fourth month, and the fast of the fifth, and the fast of the seventh, and the fast of the tenth, shall be to the house of Judah joy and gladness, and cheerful feasts; therefore love the truth and peace.

Thus saith the Lord of hosts; It shall yet come to pass, that there shall come people, and the inhabitants of many cities:

And the inhabitants of one city shall go to another, saying, Let us go speedily to pray before the Lord, and to seek the Lord of hosts: I will go also.

Yea, many people and strong nations shall come to seek the Lord of hosts in JERUSALEM, and to pray before the Lord.

Thus saith the Lord of hosts; In those days it shall come to pass, that ten men shall take hold out of all languages of the nations, even shall take hold of the skirt of him that is a Jew, saying, We will go with you: for we have heard that God is with you.

Zechariah 14:1-21:

Behold, the day of the Lord cometh, and thy spoil shall be divided in the midst of thee.

For I will gather all nations against JERUSALEM to battle; and the city shall be taken, and the houses rifled, and the women ravished; and half of the city shall go forth into captivity, and the residue of the people shall not be cut off from the city.

Then shall the Lord go forth, and fight against those nations, as when he fought in the day of battle.

And his feet shall stand in that day upon the mount of Olives, which is before JERUSALEM on the east, and the mount of Olives shall cleave in the midst thereof toward the east and toward the west, and there shall be a very great valley; and half of the mountain shall remove toward the north, and half of it toward the south.

And ye shall flee to the valley of the mountains; for the valley of the mountains shall reach unto Azal: yea, ye shall flee, like as ye fled from before the earthquake in the days of Uzziah king of Judah: and the Lord my God shall come, and all the saints with thee.

And it shall come to pass in that day, that the light shall not be clear, nor dark:

But it shall be one day which shall be known to the Lord, not day, nor night: but it shall come to pass, that at evening time it shall be light.

And it shall be in that day, that living waters shall go out from JERUSALEM; half of them toward the former sea, and half of them toward the hinder sea: in summer and in winter shall it be.

And the Lord shall be king over all the earth: in that day shall there be one Lord, and his name one.

All the land shall be turned as a plain from Geba to Rimmon south of JERUSALEM: and it shall be lifted up, and inhabited in her place, from Benjamin's gate unto the place of the first gate, unto the corner gate, and from the tower of Hananeel unto the king's winepresses.

And men shall dwell in it, and there shall be no more utter destruction; but JERUSALEM shall be safely inhabited.

And this shall be the plague wherewith the Lord will smite all the people that have fought against JERUSALEM; Their flesh shall consume away while they stand upon their feet, and their eyes shall consume away in their holes, and their tongue shall consume away in their mouth.

And it shall come to pass in that day, that a great tumult from the Lord shall be among them; and they shall lay hold every one on the hand of his neighbour, and his hand shall rise up against the hand of his neighbour.

And Judah also shall fight at JERUSALEM; and the wealth of all the heathen round about shall be gathered together, gold, and silver, and apparel, in great abundance.

And so shall be the plague of the horse, of the mule, of the camel, and of the ass, and of all the beasts that shall be in these tents, as this plague.

And it shall come to pass, that every one that is left of all the nations which came against JERUSALEM shall even go up from year to year to worship the King, the Lord of hosts, and to keep the feast of tabernacles.

And it shall be, that whoso will not come up of all the families of the earth unto JERUSALEM to worship the King, the Lord of hosts, even upon them shall be no rain.

And if the family of Egypt go not up, and come not, that have no rain; there shall be the plague, wherewith the Lord will smite the heathen that come not up to keep the feast of tabernacles.

This shall be the punishment of Egypt, and the punishment of all nations that come not up to keep the feast of tabernacles.

In that day shall there be upon the bells of the horses, Holiness Unto The Lord; and the pots in the Lord's house shall be like the bowls before the altar.

Yea, every pot in JERUSALEM and in Judah shall be holiness unto the Lord of hosts: and all they that sacrifice shall come and take of them, and seethe therein: and in that day there shall be no more the Canaanite in the house of the Lord of hosts.

Luke 2:41-51:

Now his parents went to JERUSALEM every year at the feast of the passover.

And when he was twelve years old, they went up to JERUSALEM after the custom of the feast.

And when they had fulfilled the days, as they returned, the child Jesus tarried behind in JERUSALEM; and Joseph and his mother knew not of it.

But they, supposing him to have been in the company, went a day's journey; and they sought him among their kinsfolk and acquaintance.

And when they found him not, they turned back again to JERUSALEM, seeking him.

And it came to pass, that after three days they found him in the TEMPLE, sitting in the midst of the doctors, both hearing them, and asking them questions.

And all that heard him were astonished at his understanding and answers.

And when they saw him, they were amazed: and his mother said unto him, Son, why hast thou thus dealt with us? behold, thy father and I have sought thee sorrowing.

And he said unto them, How is it that ye sought me? wist ye not that I must be about my Father's business?

And they understood not the saying which he spake unto them.

And he went down with them, and came to Nazareth, and was subject unto them: but his mother kept all these sayings in her heart.

Acts 2:1-18:

And when the day of Pentecost was fully come, they were all with one accord in one place.

And suddenly there came a sound from heaven as of a rushing mighty wind, and it filled all the house where they were sitting.

And there appeared unto them cloven tongues like as of fire, and it sat upon each of them.

And they were all filled with the Holy Ghost, and began to speak with other tongues, as the Spirit gave them utterance.

And there were dwelling at JERUSALEM Jews, devout men, out of every nation under heaven.

Now when this was noised abroad, the multitude came together, and were confounded, because that every man heard them speak in his own language.

And they were all amazed and marvelled, saying one to another, Behold, are not all these which speak Galilaeans?

And how hear we every man in our own tongue, wherein we were born?

Parthians, and Medes, and Elamites, and the dwellers in Mesopotamia, and in Judaea, and Cappadocia, in Pontus, and Asia,

Phrygia, and Pamphylia, in Egypt, and in the parts of Libya about Cyrene, and strangers of Rome, Jews and proselytes,

Cretes and Arabians, we do hear them speak in our tongues the wonderful works of God.

And they were all amazed, and were in doubt, saying one to another, What meaneth this?

Others mocking said, These men are full of new wine.

But Peter, standing up with the eleven, lifted up his voice, and said unto them, Ye men of Judaea, and all ye that dwell at JERUSALEM, be this known unto you, and hearken to my words:

For these are not drunken, as ye suppose, seeing it is but the third hour of the day.

But this is that which was spoken by the prophet Joel;

And it shall come to pass in the last days, saith God, I will pour out of my Spirit upon all flesh: and your sons and your daughters shall prophesy, and your young men shall see visions, and your old men shall dream dreams:

And on my servants and on my handmaidens I will pour out in those days of my Spirit; and they shall prophesy:

Romans 11:1-36:

I say then, Hath God cast away his people? God forbid. For I also am an ISRAELite, of the seed of Abraham, of the tribe of Benjamin.

God hath not cast away his people which he foreknew. Wot ye not what the scripture saith of Elias? how he maketh intercession to God against ISRAEL, saying,

Lord, they have killed thy prophets, and digged down thine altars; and I am left alone, and they seek my life.

But what saith the answer of God unto him? I have reserved to myself seven thousand men, who have not bowed the knee to the image of Baal.

Even so then at this present time also there is a remnant according to the election of grace.

And if by grace, then is it no more of works: otherwise grace is no more grace. But if it be of works, then is it no more grace: otherwise work is no more work.

What then? ISRAEL hath not obtained that which he seeketh for; but the election hath obtained it, and the rest were blinded.

(According as it is written, God hath given them the spirit of slumber, eyes that they should not see, and ears that they should not hear;) unto this day.

And David saith, Let their table be made a snare, and a

trap, and a stumblingblock, and a recompence unto them:

Let their eyes be darkened, that they may not see, and bow down their back alway.

I say then, Have they stumbled that they should fall? God forbid: but rather through their fall salvation is come unto the Gentiles, for to provoke them to jealousy.

Now if the fall of them be the riches of the world, and the diminishing of them the riches of the Gentiles; how much more their fulness?

For I speak to you Gentiles, inasmuch as I am the apostle of the Gentiles, I magnify mine office:

If by any means I may provoke to emulation them which are my flesh, and might save some of them.

For if the casting away of them be the reconciling of the world, what shall the receiving of them be, but life from the dead?

For if the firstfruit be holy, the lump is also holy: and if the root be holy, so are the branches.

And if some of the branches be broken off, and thou, being a wild olive tree, wert graffed in among them, and with them partakest of the root and fatness of the olive tree;

Boast not against the branches. But if thou boast, thou bearest not the root, but the root thee.

Thou wilt say then, The branches were broken off, that I might be graffed in.

Well; because of unbelief they were broken off, and thou standest by faith. Be not highminded, but fear:

For if God spared not the natural branches, take heed lest he also spare not thee.

Behold therefore the goodness and severity of God: on them which fell, severity; but toward thee, goodness, if thou continue in his goodness: otherwise thou also shalt be cut off.

And they also, if they abide not still in unbelief, shall be graffed in: for God is able to graff them in again.

For if thou wert cut out of the olive tree which is wild by nature, and wert graffed contrary to nature into a good olive tree: how much more shall these, which be the natural branches, be graffed into their own olive tree?

For I would not, brethren, that ye should be ignorant of this mystery, lest ye should be wise in your own conceits; that blindness in part is happened to ISRAEL, until the fulness of the Gentiles be come in.

And so all ISRAEL shall be saved: as it is written, There shall come out of Sion the Deliverer, and shall turn away ungodliness from Jacob:

For this is my covenant unto them, when I shall take away their sins.

As concerning the gospel, they are enemies for your sakes: but as touching the election, they are beloved for the fathers' sakes.

For the gifts and calling of God are without repentance.

For as ye in times past have not believed God, yet have now obtained mercy through their unbelief:

Even so have these also now not believed, that through your mercy they also may obtain mercy.

For God hath concluded them all in unbelief, that he might have mercy upon all.

O the depth of the riches both of the wisdom and knowledge of God! how unsearchable are his judgments, and his ways past finding out!

For who hath known the mind of the Lord? or who hath been his counseller?

Or who hath first given to him, and it shall be recompensed unto him again?

For of him, and through him, and to him, are all things: to whom be glory for ever. Amen.

Revelation 21:1-22:5:

And I saw a new heaven and a new earth: for the first heaven and the first earth were passed away; and there was no more sea.

And I John saw the holy city, new JERUSALEM, coming down from God out of heaven, prepared as a bride adorned for her husband.

And I heard a great voice out of heaven saying, Behold, the tabernacle of God is with men, and he will dwell with them, and they shall be his people, and God himself shall be with them, and be their God.

And God shall wipe away all tears from their eyes; and there shall be no more death, neither sorrow, nor crying, neither shall there be any more pain: for the former things are passed away.

And he that sat upon the throne said, Behold, I make all things new. And he said unto me, Write: for these words are true and faithful.

And he said unto me, It is done. I am Alpha and Omega, the beginning and the end. I will give unto him that is athirst of the fountain of the water of life freely.

He that overcometh shall inherit all things; and I will be his God, and he shall be my son.

But the fearful, and unbelieving, and abominable, and murderers, and whoremongers, and sorcerers, and idolaters, and all liars, shall have their part in the lake which burneth with fire and brimstone: which is the second death.

And there came unto me one of the seven angels which had the seven vials full of the seven last plagues, and talked with me, saying, Come hither, I will shew thee the bride, the Lamb's wife.

And he carried me away in the spirit to a great and high mountain, and shewed me that great city, the holy JERUSA-LEM, descending out of heaven from God,

Having the glory of God: and her light was like unto a stone most precious, even like a jasper stone, clear as crystal;

And had a wall great and high, and had twelve gates, and at the gates twelve angels, and names written thereon, which are the names of the twelve tribes of the children of ISRAEL:

On the east three gates; on the north three gates; on the south three gates; and on the west three gates.

And the wall of the city had twelve foundations, and in them the names of the twelve apostles of the Lamb.

And he that talked with me had a golden reed to measure the city, and the gates thereof, and the wall thereof.

And the city lieth foursquare, and the length is as large as the breadth: and he measured the city with the reed, twelve thousand furlongs. The length and the breadth and the height of it are equal.

And he measured the wall thereof, an hundred and forty

and four cubits, according to the measure of a man, that is, of the angel.

And the building of the wall of it was of jasper: and the city was pure gold, like unto clear glass.

And the foundations of the wall of the city were garnished with all manner of precious stones. The first foundation was jasper; the second, sapphire; the third, a chalcedony; the fourth, an emerald;

The fifth, sardonyx; the sixth, sardius; the seventh, chrysolite; the eighth, beryl; the ninth, a topaz; the tenth, a chrysoprasus; the eleventh, a jacinth; the twelfth, an amethyst.

And the twelve gates were twelve pearls: every several gate was of one pearl: and the street of the city was pure gold, as it were transparent glass.

And I saw no temple therein: for the Lord God Almighty and the Lamb are the temple of it.

And the city had no need of the sun, neither of the moon, to shine in it: for the glory of God did lighten it, and the Lamb is the light thereof.

And the nations of them which are saved shall walk in the light of it: and the kings of the earth do bring their glory and honour into it.

And the gates of it shall not be shut at all by day: for there shall be no night there.

And they shall bring the glory and honour of the nations into it.

And there shall in no wise enter into it any thing that defileth, neither whatsoever worketh abomination, or maketh a lie: but they which are written in the Lamb's book of life.

And he shewed me a pure river of water of life, clear as crystal, proceeding out of the throne of God and of the Lamb.

In the midst of the street of it, and on either side of the river, was there the tree of life, which bare twelve manner of fruits, and yielded her fruit every month: and the leaves of the tree were for the healing of the nations.

And there shall be no more curse: but the throne of God and of the Lamb shall be in it; and his servants shall serve him:

And they shall see his face; and his name shall be in their foreheads.

And there shall be no night there; and they need no candle, neither light of the sun; for the Lord God giveth them light: and they shall reign for ever and ever.

Index

Zephaniah

Books by Ruth Ward Heflin

Glory	English Edition	ISBN 1-884369-00-6	$10.00
	Spanish Edition	ISBN 1-884369-15-4	10.00
	French Edition	ISBN 1-884369-41-3	10.00
	German Edition	ISBN 1-884369-16-2	10.00
	Swedish Edition	ISBN 1-884369-38-3	10.00
	Finnish Edition	ISBN 1-884369-75-8	10.00

Revival Glory	ISBN 1-8842369-80-4	13.00
River Glory	ISBN 1-884369-87-1	13.00
Jerusalem, Zion, Israel and the Nations		
	ISBN 1-884369-65-0	13.00

Ask for them at your favorite bookstore or from:

Calvary Books
11352 Heflin Lane
Ashland, VA 23005
(804) 798-7756

www.revivalglory.org

God of Miracles
Eighty Years of the Miraculous

by Edith Ward Heflin

"My life has been very exciting because I was always looking forward to the next miracle, the next answer to prayer, the next thing Jesus would do for me. I expect I have lived twenty lifetimes within these eighty years. The God of all miracles has been so good and so very gracious to me."– Edith Heflin

As you become witness to a life that has spanned the period from Azuza Street to this next great revival, the life of a unique woman who has known the great ministries of our century and has herself lived the life of the miraculous, you too will encounter the God of Miracles.

ISBN 1-56043-043-5 $10.00

Ask for them at your favorite bookstore or from:

Calvary Books
11352 Heflin Lane
Ashland, VA 23005
(804) 798-7756
www.revivalglory.org

Hear the Voice of God

by
Wallace H. Heflin, Jr.

* Does God still speak to His people as He did to the prophets of old?
* If so, how does He speak?
* Can we actually hear His voice?
* What can we do to become more sensitive to God's voice?

Wallace Heflin Jr. spent a lifetime hearing the voice of God and following God's directives in dynamic ministry to the people of this nation and the world. In this manuscript, the last one that he prepared before his death in December of 1996, he challenges us that not only is it possible to hear the voice of God, but that God actually extends to every one of us an invitation to commune with Him.

ISBN 1-884369-36-7 $13.00

Ask for them at your favorite bookstore or from:

Calvary Books
11352 Heflin Lane
Ashland, VA 23005
(804) 798-7756
www.revivalglory.org

The Power of Prophecy

by
Wallace H. Heflin, Jr.

"Of all the nine gifts of the Spirit, prophecy is the gift that God is using most to bring in the revival of the end-time. Because of that, it is prophecy that is being opposed now more than any other gift. I want to declare that it is time to take the limits off the gift of prophecy and off the prophets God has raised up for this hour. It is time to move into God's plan of action to declare His will prophetically to this, the final generation."

– Rev. Wallace Heflin, Jr.

- What is prophecy?
- What does it accomplish?
- Who can prophesy?
- How can YOU get started prophesying?

These and many other important questions are answered in this unique and timely volume.

ISBN 1-884369-22-7 $10.00

Ask for them at your favorite bookstore or from:

Calvary Books
11352 Heflin Lane
Ashland, VA 23005
(804) 798-7756
www.revivalglory.org

Other books

by
Rev. Wallace H. Heflin, Jr.

A Pocket Full of Miracles	0-914903-23-3	7.00
Bride, The	1-884369-10-3	7.00
Jacob and Esau	1-884369-01-4	7.00
The Potter's House	1-884369-61-8	9.00
Power In Your Hand	1-884369-04-9	8.00
Power In Your Hand *(Spanish Edition)*	1-884369-04-9	6.00

Ask for them at your favorite bookstore or from:

Calvary Books
11352 Heflin Lane
Ashland, VA 23005
(804) 798-7756
www.revivalglory.org

The BESTSELLING:

GLORY

by
Ruth Ward Heflin

What is Glory?

- *It is the realm of eternity.*
- *It is the revelation of the presence of God.*
- *He is the glory! As air is the atmosphere of the Earth, so glory is the atmosphere of Heaven.*

Praise ... until the spirit of worship comes. Worship ... until the glory comes. Then ... stand in the glory. If you can capture the basic principles of praise, worship and glory which are outlined in this book – so simple that we often miss them – you can have anything else you want in God.

ISBN 1-884369-00-6 $10.00

Ask for them at your favorite bookstore or from:

Calvary Books
11352 Heflin Lane
Ashland, VA 23005
(804) 798-7756
www.revivalglory.org

The BESTSELLING:
REVIVAL GLORY

by
Ruth Ward Heflin

What is Revival Glory?

- *It is standing in the cloud and ministering directly from the cloud unto the people.*
- *It is seeing in to the eternal realm and declaring what you are seeing.*
- *It is gathering in the harvest, using only the tools of the Spirit.*
- *It is, ultimately, the revelation of Jesus Christ.*

One cannot have revival without the glory or the glory without having revival.

ISBN 1-884369-80-4 $13.00

Ask for them at your favorite bookstore or from:

Calvary Books
11352 Heflin Lane
Ashland, VA 23005
(804) 798-7756
www.revivalglory.org

The BESTSELLING:
RIVER GLORY

by
Ruth Ward Heflin

What is River Glory?

Through the analogy of the river, God has given us a whole new conciousness of His Spirit. Because He wants us to know the Spirit, He is showing us the river. When we see the Spirit of God as a great flowing river, we can better understand how to step into it and how to flow with its currents. The river is the Holy Spirit and the flow of the river is the outpouring of the Spirit. Whatever brings us to the river, if we can all get into it, every need will be supplied.

ISBN 1-884369-87-1 $13.00

Ask for them at your favorite bookstore or from:

Calvary Books
11352 Heflin Lane
Ashland, VA 23005
(804) 798-7756
www.revivalglory.org

Mount Zion Miracle Prayer Chapel

13 Ragheb Nashashibi
P.O. Box 20897
Sheikh Jarrah
Jerusalem, Israel

Tel. 972-2-5828964
Fax. 972-2-5824725
www.revivalglory.org

Prayer Meetings:

2:00 – 3:00 P.M. Daily
Monday – Thursday

Services:

Friday, Saturday and Sunday
10:30 A.M.
7:30 P.M.
Pre-meeting praise 7:00 P.M.

Come and worship with us in Jerusalem!

Calvary Pentecostal Tabernacle

11352 Heflin Lane
Ashland, VA 23005

Tel. (804) 798-7756
Fax. (804) 752-2163
www.revivalglory.org

8 ½ Weeks of Summer Campmeeting 1999
Friday, July 2 — Sunday night, August 29
With two great services daily, 11 A.M. & 8 P.M.

Ruth Heflin will be speaking nightly the first ten days and each Friday and Saturday night during Summer Campmeeting

Winter Campmeeting 2000
February 4 — 27

Ruth Heflin will be speaking nightly the first week and each Friday and Saturday night during Winter Campmeeting

Revival Meetings
Each Friday night, Saturday morning, Saturday night and Sunday night with Sister Ruth Heflin in all other months

Ministry tapes and song tapes are also available upon request.